Learning to be Literate

PEFC
PEFC/16-33-111
CATG-PEFC-052
www.pefc.org

MM Textbooks bring the subjects covered in our successful range of academic monographs to a student audience. The books in this series explore education and all aspects of language learning and use, as well as other topics of interest to students of these subjects. Written by experts in the field, the books are supervised by a team of world-leading scholars and evaluated by instructors before publication. Each text is student-focused, with suggestions for further reading and study questions leading to a deeper understanding of the subject.

Advisory Board:

Professor Colin Baker, *University of Wales, Bangor, UK*

Professor Viv Edwards, *University of Reading, Reading, UK*

Professor Ofelia García, *Columbia University, New York, USA*

Dr Aneta Pavlenko, *Temple University, Philadelphia, USA*

Professor David Singleton, *Trinity College, Dublin, Ireland*

Professor Terrence G. Wiley, *Arizona State University, Tempe, USA*

Full details of all the books in this series and of all our other publications can be found on http://www.multilingual-matters.com, or by writing to Multilingual Matters, St Nicholas House, 31–34 High Street, Bristol BS1 2AW, UK.

MM Textbooks

Consultant Editor: Professor Colin Baker

Learning to be Literate
Multilingual Perspectives

Viv Edwards

MULTILINGUAL MATTERS
Bristol • Buffalo • Toronto

Library of Congress Cataloging in Publication Data
A catalog record for this book is available from the Library of Congress.

Edwards, Viv.
Learning to be Literate: Multilingual Perspectives
Viv Edwards.
MM Textbooks: 3
Includes bibliographical references and index.
1. Education, Bilingual. 2. Literacy. 3. Multilingualism.
I. Title.
LC3719.E39 2009
370.117–dc22 2008053070

British Library Cataloguing in Publication Data
A catalogue entry for this book is available from the British Library.

ISBN-13: 978-1-84769-061-6 (hbk)
ISBN-13: 978-1-84769-060-9 (pbk)

Multilingual Matters
UK: St Nicholas House, 31–34 High Street, Bristol BS1 2AW, UK.
USA: UTP, 2250 Military Road, Tonawanda, NY 14150, USA.
Canada: UTP, 5201 Dufferin Street, North York, Ontario M3H 5T8, Canada.

The policy of Multilingual Matters/Channel View Publications is to use papers that are natural,
renewable and recyclable products, made from wood grown in sustainable forests. In the
manufacturing process of our books, and to further support our policy, preference is given to printers
that have FSC and PEFC Chain of Custody certification. The FSC and/or PEFC logos will appear on
those books where full certification has been granted to the printer concerned.

Typeset by Saxon Graphics Ltd, Derby.
Printed and bound in Great Britain by MPG Books Ltd

In memory of Hetty Edwards and for William Morriss

Dwy iaith, dwy waith y dewis
Dwa języki, podwójny wybór
Two languages, twice the choice

Dogma is narrowly monoglot.

So, if we want to stay unfooled,
let's be multilingual,
deploy the full range
of our discourse, use all our styles

Gwyneth Lewis (2007)

Contents

Acknowledgements

This book is the product of many years of observation of – and conversation with – friends who have made a considerable personal investment in raising multilingual, multiliterate children. Sincere thanks to all, but especially to Mike and Marjukka Grover, Charlotta and Tony Håggsblom, Evienia Papadaki d'Onofrio, and to Roger and Tia Sell.

Thanks in equal measure to colleagues working in this field – Colin Baker, Brigitta Busch, Eve Gregory, Frank Monaghan, Paddy Ladd, Daguo Li, 'tope Omoniyi and Naz Rassool for their unstinting support and friendship. A particular debt of gratitude, however, is owed to those colleagues I have worked most closely with at PRAESA, the University of Cape Town, for sensitizing me to the challenges of literacy teaching in Africa – Neville Alexander, Xolisa Guzula and Ntombizanele Mahobe and, above all, Carole Bloch, whose vision, determination and creativity is a source of inspiration.

Last but not least, thanks to students whose work has been used in case studies or elsewhere in the text: Shireena Basree bt Abdul Rahman, Kwasi Opoku-Amakwa, Marriote Ngwaru and An Ran. Working with you has been a pleasure and a privilege.

Multilingualism is a thread which runs through many families, including my own. Having skipped two generations, the Welsh–English 'translanguaging' which characterized conversations between my mother and grandfather has been replaced with Polish–English translanguaging. Thanks to Goska Konczak and Aga Broda for making ours a multilingual family again.

1

Reading the word, reading the world

■ This brief introductory chapter describes some of the many different ways in which children learn to be literate in two or more languages and invites you to think of other examples from your own experience.

■ It draws attention to the fragmented research on literacy in multilingual settings as disparate, for instance, as rural Zimbabwe and inner city England. While recognizing that the experiences of teachers and children can be very different, it makes a case for a more integrated approach that builds on commonalities between these various settings.

■ It discusses the scope and organization of the book.

Many routes to literacy

The title of this chapter comes from a book by Donaldo Macedo and Paulo Freire which makes links between literacy and politics: reading is not only about decoding the word from the page; it is also about the ways in which literacy can be used to empower and disempower people. This link is a recurring theme in the present book, too. The wordplay which underpins it is particularly appropriate in the context of the children in many different parts of the world who are learning read in more than one language. Let's look at some examples.

Redlands Primary School serves a highly diverse population in an inner city area of a town in southern England. Over 30 different languages are spoken. Many of the children have a parent who is studying at the university or working in the hospital nearby. The largest group, though, consists of children whose parents and grandparents arrived in the UK from Pakistan in the 1960s. The language of the home is Panjabi. Many of the children, however, are learning to read and write in Urdu, the language of literature and high culture in Pakistan, in a lunchtime club taught by one of the Redlands teachers. The introduction of an Urdu word-processing program was greeted with considerable enthusiasm by parents and children who use it for writing bilingual stories and captions for classroom displays (see Figure 1.1). These activities also attracted the attention of non-Pakistani children, several of whom started to attend the Urdu club.

Figure 1.1 Part of a classroom display of self-portraits with Urdu captions

Ikastola Errobi is a small four-class school in Cambo-les-Bains in the foothills of the Pyrenees in the northern Basque country. The teachers' salaries are paid by the French government, but the buildings and other resources are funded by a cooperative of parents, some of whom speak only French but who are anxious for their children to reclaim their Basque heritage. As part of work on narrative, children were asked to produce their own bilingual, multimedia stories in Basque – introducing the characters, setting a problem, saying what happened, providing a resolution and giving the tale a twist. They read each other's stories, voted for the best draft – *Zaunka ari zen gatua (The cat that barked)* – and then worked together on improving it. Once the Basque version was complete, the story was sent to another class, where it was translated into French. The story was then read by a class of six-year-olds with less-developed Basque language skills who drew the illustrations (see Figure 1.2).

Figure 1.2 A page from the bilingual multimedia story about *The cat that barked*

The Vulindlela Reading Club meets in Langa, a residential area established to segregate Black Africans from other racial groups in Cape Town during the apartheid era in South Africa. The club, launched in response to a request from a community organization, welcomes up to 200 children from Grades 2 to 6 from 10 to 12 on Saturday mornings. The sessions start with circle games and the singing of the Reading Club song, *Education is fun*, in English and isiXhosa. The children then divide into three different age groups to listen to stories and stretch out or cuddle up with a book. The sessions usually finish with a story telling session (See Figure 1.3). English and isiXhosa are used in the Reading Club on alternate weeks.

Figure 1.3 Stories at the Vulindlela Reading Club

Play English (see Figure 1.4) in Monza, Italy, started as a playgroup for children aged three to five. The demand was such that soon there were two separate activities, a preschool day program and an after-school program. As the first Play English pupils approached elementary school age, parents, delighted with their children's progress, exerted pressure for provision to continue. The school now covers all the elementary grades and is beginning to extend to the Middle School years. Approximately equal amounts of time are given to literacy learning in English and Italian. The academic outcomes for the children, most of whom come from Italian-speaking homes, are comparable to those of their peers attending Italian schools. But, in addition, they are able to understand, speak, read and write in English at levels far superior to children in the Italian system.

Figure 1.4 Children at Play English, Monza

The Chinese School in Reading in the south of England meets in a local primary school on Sunday mornings. It has two sections. One serves the predominantly Cantonese-speaking community that arrived in the UK in the 1950s and 1960s. The other teaches, through the medium of Mandarin or Putonghua, the official language of the People's Republic of China. Most of the children in this section are from sojourner families who stay in the UK for three or four years for study or work; they need to maintain high levels of literacy in Chinese for their return to China. Others are the children of longer-term residents from the People's Republic, whose parents are keen for them to either learn or maintain Chinese literacy skills. A smaller group consists of Cantonese speakers wishing to develop Mandarin in recognition of the importance of China on the world stage. A wall chart sets out the different stokes that make up Chinese characters. Great attention to detail is required: the strokes need to be written in a set order and the right proportions maintained (Figure 1.5).

Figure 1.5 A page from Li Wei's exercise book

Alexandra d'Onofrio is a citizen of the world. Born in London to a Greek mother and Italian father, she spent the first eight years of her life in England, attending first an Italian nursery and then the Greek Embassy School before transferring to an English primary school. The family moved briefly to Greece where Alexandra attended an Italian language-medium school before settling permanently in Italy. Throughout this time, her mother nurtured reading and writing in all three of her first languages, placing more emphasis, for instance, on Italian and English when they were in Greece, and more emphasis on English and Greek in Italy. In the early stages, she read stories and used post-its to label household objects – fridge, kettle, cupboard, table – in one language on one day, and another on the next. Alexandra returned to the UK for her higher education where she graduated with a degree in Social Anthropology and Hindi (see Figure 1.6). She later traveled to Cuba and Mexico where she learned Spanish, and spent six months in Brazil working on a Theatre of the Oppressed project where she learned Portuguese.

Pakistani and Chinese children in the south of England, Basque children in the foothills of the Pyrenees, the Vulindlela Reading Club in Cape Town, children learning in Italian and English in northern Italy, Alexandra d'Onofrio – these are all examples from my personal experience of children learning to be literate in more than one language. Readers of this book will no doubt be able to add many more examples of their own.

Figure 1.6 Alexandra d'Onofrio

The scope and organization of this book

Research on literacy learning in multilingual settings has tended to be fragmentary. The catalyst for much of this work has been the large numbers of minority language-speaking children in important migrant destinations – the US, Canada, the UK and Australia. While many researchers have been concerned with the learning of English, others have focused on the opportunities for learning through other languages in 'immersion' and bilingual education programs. Still others have looked at the voluntary efforts of minority communities to maintain their heritage languages. Although most research is concentrated in the developed world, important exceptions include the growing numbers of studies of literacy learning in South America and Africa. There are clearly differences between these various settings, but there are also many commonalities. My aim, then, is to integrate the insights from these various strands.

It may be helpful to explain the limits at the outset. This book is *not* about the considerable progress made by cognitive and developmental psychologists in exploring the literacy acquisition in bilingual children. While this research is making an invaluable contribution to our understanding of the human brain, it is often unclear how these findings can be translated into classroom practice. Nor is this a practical handbook for teachers. The focus is rather on exploring theoretical and policy issues which explain current educational practice and point to possible ways forward. As such, the book will be of interest to a wide range of people – policy-makers, researchers and practitioners – concerned with language in education.

How this book is organized

The book has three main foci: multilingualism, literacy and the management of change.

Chapters 2 and 3 explore multilingualism, the first of these three foci. Chapter 2 considers the wide range of reasons why people move from one location to another, bringing with them different languages and cultures. We examine the various accommodations made when people speaking different languages come into contact – the use of lingua francas, pidgins and creoles and the shift from one language to another. We also look at nation-building and the power relations between the majority and minority languages created in the process. Multilingualism is considered from two main perspectives: the wider society and the individual. From the perspective of the individual, we discuss the intellectual, social and economic benefits associated with speaking two or more languages. From the broader societal perspective, we challenge the assumption that multilingualism leads to division and strife and look at efforts to embrace diversity in India, South Africa and the European Union.

Chapter 3 considers how different education systems accommodate linguistically diverse populations. It does this through the lens of colonization, imperialism, nationalism and globalization, four historical processes which have each shaped the fate of diverse groups of people and their languages. It considers the educational responses to speakers of non-standard varieties, such as Black English, considered to be inferior to the standard language, and sign languages which, until recent years, were not even considered to be languages. And, finally, it examines the benefits for speakers of majority languages who elect for their children to be educated through minority languages.

The next four chapters address the second focus of the book: literacy. Chapter 4 introduces the main models developed to explain our interactions with the written word and explores the highly complex interactions between multilingualism and literacy. Drawing on the theories of Jim Cummins, it considers the conditions most likely to lead to successful literacy learning in two or more languages.

Chapter 5 looks at how literacy is taught at present and reviews the findings of research of greatest relevance for teachers. Using the example of the ongoing debate around phonics, it cautions that decisions about best practice are sometimes driven more by politics than the evidence of research; it also argues that the pedagogical implications of research in cognitive and developmental psychology are not always clear.

Chapter 6, in contrast, considers ways in which teaching might look in the future. It starts by challenging the assumption that school-based literacy is the only legitimate way to engage with the written word and shows how the children in families that share the norms and values of the school experience far less disjuncture and achieve better educational outcomes. It considers both the ways in which minorities have reacted to their marginalization in schools and children's attempts to negotiate the different approaches to literacy in school, at home and in the community. Most importantly, it explores approaches which empower students to question dominant beliefs and practices.

Chapter 7 draws attention to the shortage of reading materials suitable for use in multilingual settings and describes a range of innovations which address this need. It also focuses on the economics of minority language publishing and ways in which centralized support and co-publishing initiatives can increase the flow of materials.

Having explored possible ways forward, the final focus is on people. Although school systems are littered with failed attempts to implement change, promising models of professional development are beginning to emerge. This chapter argues for a model which addresses the what, why and how of changing teacher practice and underlines the importance of involving all stakeholders – administrators, principals, parents, teachers and children – over an extended period of time.

Each chapter ends with suggestions for further reading and lists key websites. Many of us have personal experience of learning to read and write in a second language; most of us have access to friends, family or neighbors who have developed these skills as children. For this reason, discussion points and activities offer opportunities for readers to share their own experiences and learn from fellow students.

Multilingualism

This chapter unpicks some of the complexities of multilingualism by asking key questions:

- What is a language?

- Why, on a global level, do most people speak two or more languages? We explore the environmental, scientific, economic and political developments which give rise to multilingualism.

- When groups of people speaking different languages come into contact, how do they communicate? We look at the use of lingua francas, pidgins and creoles and the decisions which lead people to shift from one language to another.

- Why are some languages more powerful than others? We examine the role which language has played in nation-building.

- What are the advantages of multilingualism for the individual? We discuss the intellectual, social and economic benefits of speaking two or more languages.

- And, finally, what are the advantages of multilingualism for the wider society? We challenge the idea that multilingualism is socially divisive and economically unviable, using examples of the ways in which governments have responded to linguistic diversity.

Language and migration

Anyone who happens to live in a predominantly English-speaking country might be forgiven for assuming that monolingualism is the normal condition. They would be wrong. In most parts of the world and for most people, multilingualism is the everyday reality. Why, then, is multilingualism so common? The answer lies in the wide range of reasons that people move from one location to another.

Environmental factors have played a part in population movement since prehistoric times. Groups in search of new grazing lands moved south and west as pastureland in Central Asia expanded or contracted with climate change (Manning, 2005). The most probable explanation for the spread of the Bantu peoples from western to central and eastern Africa is the drying of the Sahara. In modern times, a million deaths in the Irish potato starvation years of 1846–50 was an important catalyst for emigration to Britain, Australia and the USA (Kinealy, 1995).

Scientific change also drives population movement. New agricultural techniques may well have made it possible for the Bantu peoples to expand still further from central and eastern into southern Africa (Hoerder, 2002; Manning, 2005). Developments in transport allowed 50 million European migrants to move to the Americas and Australia between 1846 and 1940 and for a further 80 million to migrate across East and South Asia (McKeown, 2004).

Scientific innovation is closely linked with *economic interests*. The technological developments of the Industrial Revolution created a demand for labor which pulled the rural poor to the cities (Stearns, 2004). In modern times, globalization is exerting similar forces. As Western countries take advantage of raw materials and cheap labor in developing countries, low-skilled and female labor is migrating from the countryside to the cities (Lechner & Boli, 2004). This population movement, in turn, is giving rise to underemployment in the cities. By the same token, it is no accident that the Republic of Ireland, for centuries a 'sending country', became a 'receiving country' following the economic boom which accompanied entry into the European Union.

Economics and *politics* are, of course, close bedfellows. In the early 17th century, the East India Company was trading in spices, cotton, silk and other goods (Wild, 2000). By the 18th century, it was the chief agent of British imperialism over much of the subcontinent; by the 19th century, its activities in China were the catalyst for the expansion of British influence in East Asia. Power is an important theme not only in explorations of migration but also in discussions of language and literacy, and one to which we will be returning in subsequent chapters.

Languages in contact

While language contact has always been a feature of human communication, two recent developments suggest that this is happening on an unprecedented scale. The first concerns the current flow of people across national borders, a phenomenon that some writers are describing as 'superdiversity' or the 'diversification of diversity' (Vertovec, 2006); the second is the emergence of digital technologies which are reshaping the ways in which we communicate. People use different languages in different ways for different purposes; their levels of competence will often vary across different varieties.

When languages come into contact, the outcome depends to a large degree on local circumstances (Kerswill, 2006). For instance, is the migration over a short or long distance? Is the displacement short or long term? Have people chosen to move or were they given no choice? It is possible, however, to identify three main linguistic processes: the use of lingua francas; pidginization and creolization; and the shift from speaking one language to another.

Lingua francas

A lingua franca is used for communication between groups that come into contact in situations such as commerce, diplomacy or cultural exchanges (Knapp & Meierkord, 2002). The language used is normally the language of the most influential nation of the time. The original lingua franca was a Romance pidgin used by seafarers in the Mediterranean until the late 19th century. Various languages, however, have assumed a similar role: Greek and Latin in the Middle Ages; French in European diplomacy from the 17th to the early 20th centuries. Current examples include Mandarin (or Putonghua) in the People's Republic of China and Hausa across wide stretches of West Africa.

The most successful contemporary lingua franca, of course, is English, used on a global stage in diplomacy, international business, science and aviation (Crystal, 2003; Graddol, 2006). Its current influence can be attributed, in part, to the wide reach of the British Empire but also, and more importantly, to the economic, cultural and technological dominance of the United States.

Pidginization and creolization

Pidgins often evolve in situations of multilingual contact as, for instance, when large numbers of Africans, speaking many different languages, were transported as part of the Atlantic slave trade (Holm, 2000; Kouwenberg, 2007). Pidgins with greatly simplified grammar and vocabulary emerged making it possible for basic communication between groups of people speaking different languages. In situations of this kind, there is always a dominant language – sometimes called the lexifier – which contributes most of the vocabulary. In Jamaica, this was English, in Haiti it was French and in Surinam it was Dutch.

In the early stages, the 'pre-pidgin' is restricted in use and variable in structure. But later, a stable pidgin develops with grammatical rules quite different from the lexifier. This stable pidgin is generally learned as a second language for communication among people who speak different languages. Examples include Nigerian Pidgin and Bislama, which is spoken in Vanuatu. Over time, if the pidgin becomes the first language of subsequent generations, a process of expansion makes it possible for the resulting *creole* to serve all the communication needs of its speakers. Examples include Gullah (spoken by people of African descent in the Sea Islands and coastal areas of South Carolina, Georgia and northern Florida), Jamaican Creole and Hawai'i Creole English.

Case study: Hawai'i Creole

Hawai'i became an important stopover for European ships involved in whaling and trading with Asia in the late 18th century. The rapid expansion in the following century of the sugarcane plantations created an urgent demand for labor. Workers from as far afield as China and Portugal, Japan and Russia, needed a common language. At first, Hawaiian and Pidgin Hawaiian served this need; later in the century a new pidgin began to develop. The description which follows is based on the Hawai'i Creole web pages compiled by Ermile Hargrove, Kent Sakoda and Jeff Siegel (www.une.edu.au/langnet/definitions/hce.html).

In the 1870s immigrant families began to arrive and more children were born on the plantations. Children learned their parents' languages and were exposed to English at school. The language of the playground was influenced by the Pidgin English brought to Hawai'i earlier, by the Hawaiian spoken by their parents, and by their own first languages, especially Portuguese. By the turn of the century a new Hawai'i Pidgin English began to emerge with features from all of these sources. This pidgin became the primary language of many of those who grew up in Hawai'i, and children began to acquire it as their first language. This was the beginning of Hawai'i Creole English. By the 1920s it was the language of the majority of Hawai'ian population.

Since English is the lexifier language of Hawai'i Creole, most of the words come from English, e.g. *beef* can mean 'fight', *stink eye* means 'dirty look' and *chicken skin* means 'goose bumps'. Its sound system differs in systematic ways from English, as does its grammar. Examples of these differences include:

Sentences giving a location use *stay*:
  Da cat stay in da house
  (The cat's in the house)

No verb is required in some sentences:
  My sister skinny
  (My sister's skinny)

The verb is usually used without endings, but instead tense markers that come before the verb show when or how something happens:
  Dey wen paint his skin
  They painted his skin.

Language maintenance and shift

Another consequence of language contact is that people shift from speaking their mother tongue to the language of the dominant group (Fishman, 1991, 2001). In some cases, this shift is very rapid: in many Hispanic families in the US today, the process is complete in two to thee generations (Crawford, 2008). In other cases, change takes place much more slowly. Isolated communities, such as the Pennsylvania Dutch, have successfully transmitted their heritage language for several centuries (Haldeman, 2007).

Language shift is usually, but not invariably in one direction. In mid-20th century Wales, for instance, the Welsh language was in dramatic decline. Yet subsequent political and economic developments have helped to slow and even reverse this trend (Edwards, 2004).

Case study: The fall and rise of Welsh

When Wales was made a part of the kingdom of England in the 16th century, Welsh was excluded from the public domain. Although the gentry abandoned their mother tongue in order to make their way in public life, the lower classes continued to speak the language.

The 19th century was an important turning point. In 1850 Welsh speakers represented over 70% of the population. By 1900 they made up slightly under half. Many factors played a role in this decline, including education. A system of payment by results, for instance, which required arithmetic and reading and writing to be assessed in English, but not in Welsh, meant that there was no incentive to teach the language.

Education was not the only factor in the decline of Welsh. The mass internal migration from rural areas of Wales, as well as from England and Ireland, to the industrial valleys of south Wales disturbed traditional patterns of language use. Railways increased mobility and reduced the isolation of rural communities. The great loss of life in the First World War, together with the progressive decline in attendance at Nonconformist chapels, a traditional stronghold of the Welsh language, also helped reduce the numbers of Welsh speakers. The proportion of the population able to speak the language finally stabilized at 18.7% by the 1991 census. By the 2001 census, both the number (minimum estimate 575,604) and the percentage (about 22%) of Welsh speakers indicated that the long-standing pattern of language loss was starting to reverse.

Language activists helped to bring about this change in fortunes. Frustrated by official indifference to their arguments, they began to take more radical action, attacking TV transmitters, painting out English road signs and setting fire to the holiday homes of English incomers. The threat by Gwynfor Evans, a Welsh Nationalist Member of Parliament, to go on hunger strike finally led to the setting up of a Welsh language television channel in 1982.

The publicity generated by these activities influenced the passing of legislation to strengthen the status of Welsh. The 1967 Welsh Language Act offered 'equal validity' for English and Welsh in Wales but had only limited impact. In contrast, a much stronger act, passed in 1993, accorded Welsh and English equal status in public life and the administration of justice, and gave the Welsh Language Board responsibility for promoting the language. The devolution of power from the Westminster government in London to a Welsh National Assembly in 2000 also helped create a more favorable climate and a stronger Welsh identity.

Ironically, the only way of counteracting the rapid retreat of Welsh from more anglicized areas of the country was through schooling – the very institution that had played such an important part in undermining the language at an earlier date. In 2002, one in five primary school children was being taught in classes where Welsh was used either as the main medium of education or for teaching part of the curriculum. Much of the increase in both the numbers and proportion of Welsh speakers reported in the 2001 census can be attributed to bilingual education, with three-quarters of the primary school children fluent in the language coming from English-speaking homes.

There is, however, no room for complacency. Four in every ten children who complete their primary school education through the medium of Welsh go on to English-medium secondary education. The same proportion of Welsh-speaking adults report that they lack confidence in speaking the language.

Languages and nation-building

In discussing what happens when languages come into contact, we touched on the issue of dominant languages. The relationships between majority (or dominant) and minority (or subordinate) languages are complex: how, for instance, can the same language be a majority language in one setting (e.g. German in Germany and Austria) and a minority language in others (e.g. German in Denmark and Poland)? The answer to this question lies in an understanding of nation-building and nationalism (May, 2001; Wright, 2004). The story begins in Europe, the birthplace of the modern nation state and extends to most other continents.

In medieval Europe, dynasties acquired land through conquest, dowry and inheritance. The ruling classes were multilingual actors on a large geographical stage. In contrast, most of their monolingual subjects spoke a dialect of one of several branches of the Indo-European family of languages (Wright, 2004). Because the masses lived where they were born and died, the speech of each small community differed only in small respects from the speech of its neighbors.

During this period, territories changed hands frequently. Political instability offered few opportunities to develop allegiance to one particular group or one way of speaking. In simple terms, there was no majority by which to define minorities and ruling elites took little interest in the language of their subjects.

With the religious conflicts in the 16th and 17th centuries, rulers in Spain, Portugal, France, Britain, Sweden, Denmark and the Netherlands began to fix the limits of their territories. Prior to the Reformation, a worshipper's relationship with God was mediated by the clergy, the only people able to read the Latin Bible. Protestants, however, wanted to be able to read the Bible for themselves, and thus created a demand for translations in local languages making it possible for printers to reach large markets; these Bible translations, in turn, consolidated the influence of local languages.

The absolute monarchs of this period imposed their will through multilingual bureaucracies. As their right to rule was challenged, other linguistic solutions took precedence. State bureaucracy, urbanization and, in some cases, revolution all helped to reinforce the notion of 'one language, one nation'. For instance, following the French Revolution, the use of French became a patriotic duty. Such ideologies were highly effective in promoting French in a country where as few as three out of 31 million people spoke the language fluently at the end of the 18th century.

The 19th century witnessed a new wave of nation states, based on an attachment to a common past rather than to dynasties. The area later to become Germany, for example, consisted of some 350 small states and cities. To justify the new political entity, leaders drew on myths about the historic westward movement of Teutonic tribes, conveniently disregarding religious and cultural differences among their descendants. Later, from the 1880s to the start of the First World War, European economic interests led to the arbitrary carving up of Africa into future nation states with scant attention to ethnic boundaries (Rassool *et al.*, 2007).

The creation of nation states was an untidy process (May, 2001). While the *state* is a political and geopolitical entity, the *nation* is a cultural or ethnic entity. The only nation state where it might be argued that citizens share a common language, culture and values is Iceland. Elsewhere the drive for national cohesion through loyalty to a single language and culture has led to the creation of linguistic minorities.

In recent times, the supremacy of nation states has been being challenged by supranational developments, including cross-border flows of investments, services and ideas. There is a similar transnational flow of languages (Edwards, 2004). In the 2001 Canadian census, one in every six people reported a home language other than English or French; more than 100 different languages were recorded. The 2001 Australian census reported that 142 languages, in addition to Aboriginal languages, were spoken by just over one in six of the population. According to the 2000 US census, the proportion of people speaking a home language other than English was even higher: one in five. In the UK, over 300 different languages were recorded in a 2000 survey of London schoolchildren. Language is one indicator of 'superdiversity', the defining feature of the late 20th and 21st centuries.

What is a language anyway?

All of the discussion so far has been based on the assumption that we have a shared understanding of 'language'. This is not necessarily the case. For instance, what is the difference between a language and a dialect?

Dialects are usually considered to be a subset of a language. As we saw in the discussion of nation-building in Europe, they form continua with only slight modifications from one location to the next. While speakers on adjacent points can understand each other, those at the far ends of the continua may well experience problems of mutual intelligibility. A single dialect continuum often gives rise to several languages, and decisions about the boundaries can be contentious. Danish, Swedish and Norwegian, for instance, all belong to the same Nordic dialect continuum; their speakers consider them to be separate languages, mirroring the political autonomy of the three nations. Interestingly, the linguistic distance between these three 'languages' is far less than the differences associated with the 'dialects' of Chinese or Arabic: here, the political imperative is to emphasize commonalities between different peoples. Examples of this kind demonstrate very clearly that decisions about languages and dialects are determined more by politics than linguistics. In the words of a Yiddish saying: 'A language is a dialect with an army and a navy'.

In the process of nation-building, government policies address not only which languages will be used for official purposes, but which varieties of these languages. Power relationships invariably prevail. In England, standard English was based on the East Midlands variety spoken in the triangle enclosed by the seats of learning, Oxford and Cambridge, and London, the commercial heartland of the nation (Baugh & Cable, 2001). In France, standard French is similarly associated with Parisian speech and the seat of power (Nadeau & Barlow, 2008). Standard Modern Greek is based on the variety spoken around Athens. The use of standard varieties protects the interests and influence of a small but powerful elite and marginalizes other groups in the process.

Issues concerning standardization extend beyond national boundaries (Edwards, 2007a). In the UK, for instance, most Greek-speaking children speak the Cypriot variety rather than Standard Modern Greek; most children of Italian heritage speak a southern variety; most Bangladeshi children speak Sylheti and not Bengali, the national language; and many Muslim Panjabi-speaking children, like the children in Redlands Primary School in Chapter 1, will choose to read and write in Urdu, the language of religion and high culture in Pakistan, rather than Panjabi, the language of the home. In learning to read and write in minority languages, the issue thus becomes which variety should be used.

While non-standard varieties are often grudgingly considered to be inferior versions of the standard, *sign languages* are treated with even greater contempt (Ladd, 2003). For over a century, educationalists outlawed sign, placing exclusive emphasis on the use of speech, irrespective of the degree of children's hearing loss. More recently, attitudes have begun to change. It is now understood that sign languages are able to express the same range of functions and the same level of nuance as spoken languages. They have been accorded official recognition in a growing number of countries including Belgium, the UK, Ireland and Aotearoa/New Zealand.

Writers such as Pennycook and Makoni (2007) react to this fuzziness around language by arguing that languages are inventions: they simply don't exist as separate objects or entities that can be classified and counted. It is certainly the case that Western notions of language carry little or no meaning in many societies. For instance, when mapping the boundaries between the languages and dialects of India, Grierson (1928) was confronted with the inconvenient truth that, while the 'natives' were conversant with the notion of dialect, they struggled to understand 'language'. Language names such as Bengali and Assamese were imposed by European linguists. Further clues as to the invented nature of language lie in the enormous disparity between linguists' estimates of the numbers of languages spoken in the world today (in the region of 7000) and the 40,000 names reported in Ethnologue, the language database of the Summer Institute of Linguistics.

The challenge to the static notion of 'a language' also has implications for discussions of multilingualism: if 'a language' is a thing, then logically bilingualism involves two and multilingualism two or more such things. How then do we explain the fact that people have differing levels of proficiency in different languages? In the code-switching between one language and another that regularly takes place when bilinguals converse, at what point do we assign an utterance to one language rather than another? The confusion around terms such as first language and mother tongue is another symptom of this fuzziness. Mother tongue, for instance, may seem at first glance a relatively straightforward concept but often poses serious problems for bilinguals. Indians required to supply the names of their mother tongues for census returns have been known to supply different language names from one census to the next. The eight scenarios outlined by Mallikarjun (2001) illustrate the complexities.

> **Case study:** My mother tongue is pink
>
> 1. Father and mother speak Tamil between themselves but English to their child. What is the mother tongue of the child?
> 2. Though father and mother are native speakers of a variety of Tamil, they prefer to talk to each other using Kannada. They speak to their child in that variety of Tamil on some occasions, and in Kannada on others. What is the mother tongue of the child?
> 3. Father speaks Bengali. Mother speaks Tamil. Parents use their respective languages with the child. The child acquires both languages. Can there be more than one mother tongue for an individual?
> 4. Father and mother are of Tamil origin but do not speak Tamil. They use the language of the area to speak to the child and the child acquires only that language. The child claims Tamil as her mother tongue for reasons of identity. Is it possible to claim a mother tongue she cannot speak?
> 5. Father and mother speak Telugu at home, but Tamil outside. Both speak to the child in Telugu and the child also acquires Tamil, the language of the wider community. Can there be more than one mother tongue?
> 6. The child acquires Tamil at home but soon her competence in the language spoken outside the home is greater than her competence in Tamil. Is it possible to have different mother tongues at different stages?
> 7. Some people claim Sanskrit, a classical language no longer widely spoken, as their mother tongue. Does a language need to be spoken to be claimed as a mother tongue?
> 8. Muslim families with a Tamil or Malayalam background may claim Urdu as their mother tongue for religious considerations. Can non-linguistic reasons, such as caste, religion, region or profession be used in decisions about mother tongues?
>
> An Indian friend found a way of neatly side stepping these issues. When asked as a ten-year-old what his mother tongue was, he replied: 'Pink'!

Writers such as Baker (2003) and García (2008) bypass the problems of treating languages as separable entities by using the term 'translanguaging' to describe multilingual communication. The large-scale movement of people and the rapid exchange of information, both hallmarks of the 21st century, provide a perfect backdrop for people to hone the skills involved. Unlike earlier mass migrations, people are able to stay in touch with members of the families they leave behind through phone calls, email, chat rooms and air travel. Different generations of the same family may have arrived at different times; mixed marriages and divorces add extra layers of complexity. In school, children from the same language community may have been born in the new location; alternatively they may have arrived at multiple points. In settings such as classrooms and family meals, individuals may find themselves using several languages to varying degrees and for distinct purposes in order to ensure everyone is included. Moving between TV channels and surfing the Internet call for similar translanguaging skills.

Multilingualism and the individual

The ways in which people become multilingual vary a great deal (Baker, 2006). The informal acquisition of languages in early childhood is often simultaneous. This happens, for instance, in families where one parent uses one language and the other a second language (Barron-Hauwaert, 2004). Sequential (or consecutive) bilingualism, in contrast, is associated with later childhood or adulthood where formal education is likely to play a more important role.

Another important distinction concerns elective and circumstantial bilingualism (Baker, 2006). Elective bilinguals tend to learn high-status languages. This path leads to additive bilingualism where the addition of a second language takes place at no cost to the first. Migrants and refugees, on the other hand, are circumstantial bilinguals who need new languages for survival purposes and whose first languages are often viewed in very negative terms. This course of events often leads to language shift from minority to majority languages, a process known as subtractive bilingualism. There is, of course, no reason why multilingualism should be an asset in some communities and not in others. As we will see in Chapter 3, the educational implications of subtractive bilingualism are far-reaching, with elective bilinguals consistently outperforming circumstantial bilinguals.

Whichever route to multilingualism individuals may have taken, the benefits fall into two main categories: the intellectual, and the social and economic.

Intellectual advantages

Until the 1960s, researchers claimed that children who spoke two languages found themselves at an intellectual disadvantage, performing at a lower level than monolinguals on a range of tasks (Baker, 2006; May *et al.*, 2006). These claims, however, have not stood up to close scrutiny. On some occasions, researchers were comparing middle-class monolinguals with working-class bilinguals; any differences in performance might therefore be attributable to social class. On other occasions, researchers failed to take into account that they were comparing monolinguals with bilinguals working in their weaker language. Discrepancies in performance were often explained using the image of the brain as a receptacle with a finite capacity: because two languages were assumed to take twice the space of one, bilinguals could not be expected to do as well as monolinguals.

Since the 1960s, however, a growing body of research has challenged such assumptions. The current consensus is that, instead of separate underlying proficiency in first and subsequent languages, there is, in fact, a common underlying proficiency (see Figure 2.1).

The receptacle metaphor has been replaced with the double-peaked iceberg (see Figure 2.2). The two peaks showing above the water represent the relatively automatized surface features – basic grammar, vocabulary and phonology – of the languages in question. The shared base lying below the surface represents the common underlying proficiency involved in cognitively demanding tasks. Children who, for instance, learn to read and write in Spanish do not simply have skills in Spanish; they also develop skills related to literacy which they are able to transfer when they learn to read and write another language.

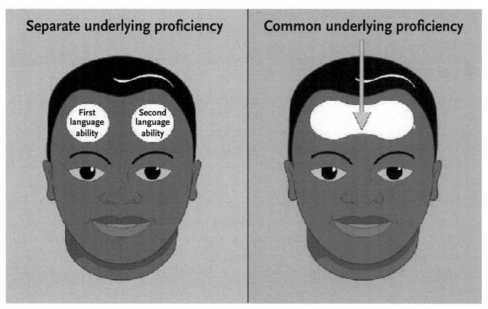

Figure 2.1 Common underlying proficiency

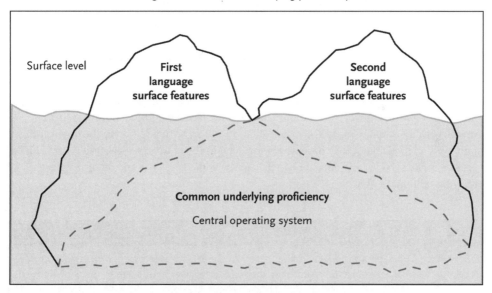

Figure 2.2 The iceberg analogy

Far from being disadvantaged, multilinguals have been shown to have advantages over monolinguals on a variety of cognitive and metacognitive tasks (Jessner, 2006). Their performance on tasks such as counting the number of words in sentences and judging the grammaticality of anomalous sentences suggests that they have higher levels of metalinguistic awareness, allowing them to focus on the form rather than the meaning of language. There is also evidence of greater sensitivity to the social nature and communicative functions of language. Finally, psychologists point to the greater mental flexibility of bilinguals, and speculate that this may be because control of two symbolic systems offers more than one way to approach a problem.

Social and economic benefits

Equally, multilingualism is associated with a range of social benefits (Edwards, 2004). Communication is, for instance, crucial to family relationships. When grandparents or parents have limited competence in the majority language and children have difficulty with the minority language, neither generation can make itself understood. Lack of fluency places a strain on all concerned in many situations. Children feel embarrassed when they can't relate to others of their own age on visits to the home country, or when they can't join in conversations with visitors.

Closely linked to communication in the family is the role of language in personal identity (Blackledge, 2004; Norton, 2000). Each language is imbued with cultural values that shape self-awareness, identity and relationships. Young people who speak the heritage language are able to explore their roots – literature, art, music, history – and have a firmer sense of who they are.

Children respond to bilingualism in different ways. Some resolve to use only the dominant language when they have children of their own. Others feel the same level of commitment as their parents to bringing up their own children to speak the minority language. Still others initially rebel against the minority language only to rediscover their identity in late adolescence or early adulthood, as part of a conscious rejection of attempts by majority language speakers to disparage them and their culture.

Multilingualism is also associated with economic benefits for the individual. In an increasingly globalized world, multilinguals bring considerable linguistic and cultural 'capital' with them to the job market (Bourdieu, 1991, 1997). In addition to the opportunities in international business, they have a growing edge in the domestic market in areas such as tourism, social services and education, particularly where there is a customer interface requiring bilingual skills.

Case study: Child language brokers

The children of parents with limited proficiency in the majority language are often thrust into adult roles at an early age, helping out in situations such as bank transactions, doctor's appointments and parent–teacher meetings. The level of sophistication shown by young children was demonstrated very clearly by Nigel Hall (2003) in a simulation where nine-year-old Urdu speakers were asked to act as interpreters for a non-English-speaking mother wanting to enroll her child in school. The child often modified what the other two participants said. For instance, at one point the mother was not impressed with the teacher's explanation of what her child would be doing in school.

Mother:	*What do they do in school?*
Child:	What do you do in school?
Teacher:	When the children are young we like them to play a lot.

Child:	*When the child is young they make them play.*
Mother:	*Not playing! Do we send our children to learn to read and write or play?*
Teacher:	What's she saying? What's she saying?
Child:	She doesn't want him to play a lot.
Teacher:	Don't worry it's playing with things to help them to learn.
Child:	*They learn him something. They learn through play, then they learn something.*
Mother:	*Oh, all right then.*

The child glosses over the mother's annoyance and thus sidesteps the problem of having to explain to one adult that another adult disagrees with them.

Multilingualism and society

There is a widespread assumption that multilingualism is a problem for the wider society. Those who advocate the use of one dominant variety as a unifying force believe that multilingualism leads to division and strife. It is possible to argue, however, that such fears are unfounded. Language is the tool and not the cause of conflict, and attempts to eliminate diversity are likely to give rise to the very tensions that proponents of monolingualism are seeking to avoid.

Complaints about the expense of interpreting and translation services in multilingual settings are also commonplace. In the context of the European Union, for instance, there is considerable debate about the trade-off between equal treatment and economic efficiency. The cost of translating tens of thousands of documents every year and of providing interpreting services for the European Parliament is high; it also leads to delays in the decision-making process. It is important, though, to see these costs in context: the translation budget in 2007 was around EUR 302 million, which represents a cost to each citizen of around EUR 0.63 a year (Europa, 2006). Concerns have also been raised about the costs of translation and interpretation for immigrants. In this case, expenditure needs to be seen in the context both of human rights and of the benefits of social inclusion (Edwards, 2004). The cost of remedying medical complications resulting from wrong diagnosis when no interpreter is available is likely to be far higher than providing interpreter services. Similarly, the price tag associated with unrest when some people are unable to meaningfully participate in society far exceeds the cost of the translation of election materials.

In spite of some dissenting voices, there is a growing understanding of the societal benefits of multilingualism (Edwards, 2004). In international trade, bilingual intermediaries, trusted by both parties, are able to offer a competitive edge. Companies are beginning to realize that ethnic communities represent important markets in themselves, and bilinguals are proving invaluable in reaching these new markets in culturally appropriate ways. Bilingual skills are equally important in the fields of diplomacy and defence.

Majority language speakers also benefit from linguistic diversity. Advantages include access to an astonishing range of cultural experiences – musical performances, subtitled films and drama, dual language books for children, to name just a few. But perhaps the most exciting by-product of diversity is the creativity it generates. Take, for instance, bilingual theatre, a new and different genre with its own devices and its own aesthetics (Tse, 2000), or the fusion of electronic and other influences with traditional music (Edwards, 2004).

Language policy and planning

State responses to multilingualism vary a great deal. At one end of the spectrum, linguistic diversity is perceived as a problem to be solved. When Ataturk came to power in Turkey in 1923, all languages other than Turkish were suppressed (Skutnabb-Kangas, 2000). While the smaller Armenian community was massacred, extermination was not practical for the 13 million Kurds, many of whom were forcibly resettled in the major cities. The Kurdish language was outlawed in public places, in education and in government offices. At the other end of the spectrum, the South African Constitution guarantees equal status to 11 official languages.

The extent of diversity varies considerably from one area to the next; so do institutional policies developed in response to diversity. The examples which follow focus on India, the European Union and South Africa. The Indian and EU case studies give a flavor of the range of issues which arise and the kinds of solutions which have been proposed. The South African case study considers how language policies are implemented in a particular service setting – public libraries.

Case study: India

Enumerators in the most recent census recorded the names of 6,661 mother tongues offered by respondents. Even after 'thorough linguistic scrutiny, edit and rationalization', the final tally of mother tongues spoken by 10,000 or more people was 122 (Census of India, 2001). So what policies are in place to deal with diversity on this scale?

Hindi and English operate as official languages at the level of central government but individual states have the freedom to decide which languages to use for internal administration and education. For instance, Telugu is the official language of Andhra Pradesh and Malayalam is the official language of Kerala. In addition, some 22 languages have gained regional status on the grounds that they are spoken by very large numbers of people. Political pressure also plays a part. For instance, two recently recognized regional languages – Manipuri/Maithei and Bodo – have fewer than 2 million speakers while Bhili/Bhiladi (with 9.6 million speakers) and Santali (with 6.5 million speakers) have yet to gain official recognition.

Because linguistic boundaries are never a perfect match with administrative boundaries, a significant proportion of the population in each state speaks the dominant language of the neighboring state. Thus, while Telugu is the main language in Andhra Pradesh, there are also sizeable communities who speak Kannada, Marathi, Oriya and Tamil, the official languages of the adjoining states.

Most Indians speak their home language and the regional or state language (where this is different from the home language); many people are also able to communicate in Hindi and English. Domain

---

has an important influence on language choice: people may speak one language at home, a second in the wider neighborhood and the market, and a third in formal situations such as education and administration.

Although in theory the states recognize one language for official purposes, in practice other languages are often used in districts where a linguistic minority constitutes 15–20% of the total population. In the state of Kerala, for instance, Malayalam and English are the official languages, but Tamil and Kannada minorities are able to use their languages for correspondence with the state government; Tamil and Kannada are also used as media of instruction in the school system in districts where there are significant populations speaking these minority languages.

Case study: The European Union

With its 27 member states and 23 official languages, the EU faces both practical and political challenges. A Commissioner for Multilingualism has the brief to encourage language learning; promote a healthy multilingual economy; to give citizens access to EU legislation in their own languages. Language rights are so politically sensitive, however, that decisions about language use tend to be left to market forces. In theory, all official languages have equal status. In reality, some languages are more 'international' than others and there is a growing reliance on English and, to a lesser extent French, as working languages.

The 23 official languages of the European Union are simply the tip of the iceberg (see Table 2.1). The EU principle of respect for other languages laid out in the 2000 Charter of Fundamental Rights applies also to the many regional and lesser-used languages which have survived in spite of the imposition of national languages. Because borders are political constructs which pay scant regard to linguistic realities, the same language sometimes has different status in different countries: Danish is the official language of Denmark, but a minority language in Germany. In other cases, a minority language is spoken within the frontiers of a single nation state, as is the case for Welsh in the UK and Breton in France. Minority languages vary from relative 'giants' such as Catalan, with its seven million speakers in France and Spain, to the estimated 2000 speakers of Saterfrisian in Germany.

The regional and lesser-used languages of Europe are protected by two pieces of legislation coordinated by the Council of Europe, a separate organization of more than 40 European states formed to promote European unity. The first of these, the European Charter for Regional or Minority Languages, is 'intended to ensure, as far as is reasonably possible, that regional or minority languages are used in education and in the media, to permit and encourage their use in legal and administrative contexts, in economic and social life, for cultural activities and in transfrontier exchanges'. The second, the Framework Convention for National Minorities also makes reference to linguistic freedoms, including use of the minority language in private and in public as well as its use with administrative authorities.

The minority languages spoken by migrant populations in the EU are not, of course, limited to regional languages. A survey of London schools (Baker & Eversley, 2000), showed that over 300 languages, many of relatively recent provenance, were spoken by more than 850,000 children. One hundred and ten different languages were reported in a similar survey of schools in The Hague in the Netherlands (van der Avoird et al., 2001). These languages are not included in the Council of Europe legislation.

Table 2.1 Languages of the European Union

Member states	Official languages
Austria, Belgium, Bulgaria, *Cyprus*, *Czech Republic*, Denmark, *Estonia*, *Finland*, France, Germany, Greece, *Hungary*, Ireland, Italy, *Latvia*, Lithuania, Luxembourg, *Malta*, Netherlands, *Poland*, Portugal, *Romania*, Slovakia, *Slovenia*, Spain, Sweden, UK	*Bulgarian*, Czech, Danish, Dutch, English, *Estonian*, Finnish, French, German, Greek, *Hungarian*, Italian, Irish, *Latvian*, *Lithuanian*, Maltese, Polish, Portuguese, *Romanian*, *Slovak*, *Slovene*, Spanish, *Swedish*

Language family	Branch	Minority and regional languages
Indo-European	Romance	Aragonese, Aroumanian, Asturian, Castilian, Catalan, Corsican, Francoprovençal, French, *Friulan*, Galician, Italian, *Ladin*, *Occitan*, *Oïl*, Portuguese, *Mirandes*, Romanian, Sardinian, Wallon
	Germanic	Danish, Dutch, English, Faroese, Frisian, German, Luxembourgish, Northern-Frisian, Saterfrisian, Swedish, Scots, Mocheno, Cimbri
	Celtic	Breton, Cornish, Irish, Manx, Gaelic, Welsh
	Slavic	Bielorussian, Bulgarian, Kashubian, Croatian, Czech, Polish, Pomak, Ruthenian, Serbian, Macedonian, Slovak, Slovene, Serbsina, Sorbian, Ukrainian
	Baltic	Latvian, Lithuanian
	Albanian	Albanian, Arvanite
	Greek	Greek
	Turkish	Tatar, Turkish
Non-Indo-European	Finn-Ugric	Estonian, Finnish, Hungarian, Sami, Livonian
	Other	Basque

Case study: Policy into practice: the case of South Africa

In South Africa a two-plus-one formula - English and Afrikaans ('two') plus an African language ('one') – must always be applied. The Batho Pele White Paper (1997) discusses the basic principles which should guide the implementation of this policy; the challenge is then for service providers to translate these principles into practice. Du Plessis (2003) sets out below how multilingualism can be used by public institutions such as libraries to improve service delivery.

The White Paper stresses the importance of multilingual communication – spoken and written – with the public and suggests a framework (see Table 2.2) for considering how this can best be achieved in the area of service delivery.

Table 2.2 Batho Pele principles and modes of language usage

	Spoken	*Written*
Discussion	Client recordings Interviews Consultation groups Meetings	Client recordings Reports
Service standards		Rules Claim forms Documents (e g IDs) Letters
Courtesy	Personal interaction with the public Telephonic contact	Letters
Information	Verbal information Toll-free telephonic contact	Graphic material Written communication Notices
Openness and transparency		Annual reporting to citizens
Correction of mistakes	Personal complaints Telephonic complaints	Written complaints
Value for money	Conversation with clients Conversation with personnel	

The underlying premise here is that the client's language preference has a high priority; there is also an assumption that the more direct the contact with the client, the more multilingual the service. Figure 2.3 demonstrates this principle.

This analysis would suggest that the minimum requirements for spoken communication in a setting such as a public library would be that:

- personnel appointments will accommodate the language variety of the particular public;
- personnel placement will be managed in a language-sensitive way;
- counter personnel and phone operators, at least, will have multilingual skills;
- a whisper-interpreting service be used on occasions where more people are involved (e.g. at meetings);
- a phone-interpreting service is used in other cases.

Similarly, the minimum requirements for written communication are that:

- public documents are translated as a matter of course;
- all proforma documentation (such as forms) will be made available in the language of the client;
- signs and instructions will be in the languages of clients;
- a system will be implemented for the handling of letters in the languages of the clients;
- the latest technology for computer-assisted translation will be utilized as far as possible.

In the case of both written and spoken communication, the institution clearly needs to budget for this kind of service delivery.

Key points

Multilingualism is the result of population movement which, in turn, is driven by many different factors including environmental change, scientific advances, politics and economics.

When different languages come into contact there are three possible consequences:

1. People use a lingua franca, normally the language of the most influential language of the day.

2. A pidgin, or a simplified form of speech is used, usually a mixture of two or more languages, with a rudimentary grammar and vocabulary. If the pidgin is used as the first language of subsequent generations, the grammar and vocabulary are expanded to a creole that meets all the communication needs of the speakers.

3. People shift from speaking their mother tongue to the language of the dominant group.

The nation-building that began in 19th century Europe was responsible for the notion of one state, one language. One language was given priority over the others spoken within the national border, creating many linguistic minorities in the process. More recently, the supremacy of nation states has been challenged by the supranational developments associated with globalization.

Individuals who speak two or more languages have intellectual, social and economic advantages over monolinguals.

Multilingualism also offers social, cultural and economic benefits for the wider society. State responses vary a great deal: there are many different models for managing linguistic diversity, from the repression of Kurdish by Turkey to the equal status guaranteed for the 11 official languages in the constitution of South Africa.

Activities and discussion points

1. Many of us have experience of migration, either personally or through a family member. As an individual, small group or class activity, plot the journeys made by yourself and family members on a world map.

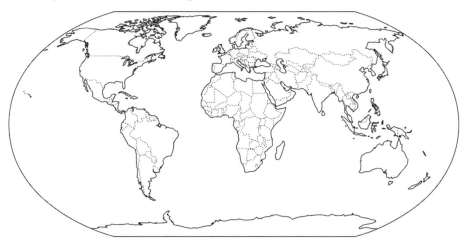

2. A language biography explores how a speaker has acquired and used their different languages. If you speak two or more languages, write your own biography; alternatively, write a language biography for someone that you know.

3. Think of the country where you live now or a country where you have lived in the past. Here are some questions to consider when discussing patterns of language use:

- Which languages are heard on a daily basis?

- How do people speaking different languages communicate with each other?

  ○ Do they use a lingua franca?

  ○ Do they use a world language?

- Is there a high degree of individual bilingualism?

- Are there language-shift trends?

Further reading

General

Edwards, V. (2004) *Multilingualism in the English-speaking World: Pedigree of Nations*. Oxford: Blackwell.

Baker, C. (2006) *Foundations of Bilingualism and Bilingual Education*. Clevedon: Multilingual Matters.

Ethnologue: www.ethnologue.com
An encyclopedic reference work cataloging the world's known living languages of the world.

Linguasphere Observatory: www.langtag.com
Register of the World's Languages and Speech Communities, covering over 20,000 varieties of language and over 70,000 linguistic and ethnic names.

Migration

Hoerder, D. (2002) *Cultures in Contact: World Migrations in the Second Millennium*. Durham, NC: Duke University Press.

Manning, P. (2005) *Migration in World History*. London: Routledge.

Language contact

Appel, R. & Muysken, P. (2006) *Language Contact and Bilingualism*. Amsterdam: Amsterdam University Press.

Kerswill, P. (2006) Migration and Language. In K. Mattheier, U. Ammon & P. Trudgill (eds) *Sociolinguistics. An International Handbook of the Science of Language and Society* (2nd edn) Vol 2. Berlin: De Gruyter.

Clyne, M. (2007) *Dynamics of Language Contact*. Cambridge: Cambridge University Press.

Winford, D. (2006) *An Introduction to Contact Linguistics*. Oxford and New Malden, MA: Blackwell.

Pidgins and creoles

Holm, J. (2000) *An Introduction to Pidgins and Creoles*. Cambridge: Cambridge University Press.

Kouwenberg, S. (2007) *Handbook of Pidgins and Creoles*. Oxford: Blackwell.

Mufwene, S. (2001) *The Ecology of Language Evolution*. Cambridge: Cambridge University Press.

Language varieties: www.une.edu.au/langnet/index.html
This site is about varieties of language that differ from the standard variety that is normally used in the media and taught in the schools. These include pidgins, creoles, regional dialects, minority dialects and indigenized varieties.

Lingua francas

Knapp, K. & Meierkord, C. (eds) (2002) *Lingua Franca Communication*. Frankfurt am Main: Peter Lang.

Crystal, D. (2003) *English as a Global Language*. Cambridge: Cambridge University Press.

Graddol, D. (2006) *English Next*. London: The British Council. Retrieved from: www.britishcouncil.org/learning-research-englishnext.htm.

Language maintenance and shift

Bradley, D. (2002) *Language Endangerment and Language Maintenance: An Active Approach*. London: RoutledgeCurzon.

Fishman, J. (2001) *Can Threatened Languages Be Saved: Reversing Language Shift, Revisited: A 21st Century Perspective.* Clevedon: Multilingual Matters.

Linguistic decline and death

Harrison, K.D. (2007) *When Languages Die: The Extinction of the World's Languages and the Erosion of Human Knowledge.* Oxford: Oxford University Press.

Romaine, S. & Nettle, D. (2000) *Vanishing Voices: The Extinction of the World's Languages.* Oxford: Oxford University Press.

Skutnabb-Kangas, T. (2000) *Linguistic Genocide in Education – or Worldwide Diversity and Human Rights?* Mahwah, NJ: Lawrence Erlbaum.

Language and nation

Wright, S. (2004) *Language Policy and Language Planning: From Nationalism to Globalization.* Basingstoke: Macmillan Palgrave.

Cognitive advantages of bi-/multilingualism

Jessner, U. (2006) *Linguistic Awareness in Multilinguals.* Edinburgh: Edinburgh University Press.

Bialystok, E. (2001) *Bilingualism in Development: Language, Literacy, and Cognition.* Cambridge: Cambridge University Press.

Bialystok, E. (2007) Acquisition of Literacy in Bilingual Children: A Framework for Research. *Language Learning* 57 (1): 45–77.

Language planning

Wright, S. (2004) *Language Policy and Language Planning: From Nationalism to Globalization.* Basingstoke: Macmillan Palgrave.

Liddicoat, A. (ed.) (2007) *Language Planning and Policy: Issues in Language Planning and Literacy.* Clevedon: Multilingual Matters.

Rassool, N., Canvin, M., Heugh, K. & Mansoor, S. (2007) *Global issues in Language, Education and Development.* Clevedon: Multilingual Matters.

Pan South African Language Board: www.pansalb.org.za
The Pan South African Language Board (PanSALB) promotes multilingualism in South Africa by fostering the development of all 11 official languages, while encouraging the use of the many other languages spoken in the country.

Welsh Language Board: www.bwrdd-yr-iaith.org.uk
Useful background information about the Welsh language and about the Welsh Language Board and its work.

Foras na Gaeilge: http://www.gaeilge.ie/
The website of the island of Ireland language body for anyone interested in any aspect of the Irish language.

Multilingualism in Europe

Ammon, U. (2006) Language Conflicts in the European Union. On Finding a Politically Acceptable and Practicable Solution for EU Institutions that Satisfies Diverging Interests. *International Journal of Applied Linguistics* 16 (3): 319–38.

Craith, M. (2005) *Europe and the Politics of Language: Citizens, Migrants and Outsiders.* Basingstoke: Palgrave Macmillan.

Phillipson, R. (2003) *English-Only Europe? Challenging Language Policy.* London & New York: Routledge.

Websites

Mercator: www.ciemen.org/mercator/
A website on linguistic rights and legislation within the European Union.

European Bureau for Lesser-Used Languages
www.eblul.org
A website promoting European linguistic
diversity.

Eurolang®: www.eurolang.net
A specialist niche news agency covering
topics related to lesser-used languages,
linguistic diversity, stateless nations and
national minorities within the European
Union.

Education in multilingual societies

The policies and practices of dominant groups have far-reaching implications for the education of minorities. In this chapter we look at:

- The ways in which education has been used both to weaken minority languages and to help reverse language shift through the lens of four historical policies and practices: *colonialism, imperialism, nationalism and globalization*

- Educational responses to speakers of marginalized languages: non-standard varieties, such as Black English that are considered to be inferior to the standard language and sign languages which, until recent years, were not even considered to be languages.

- The benefits which accrue to speakers of majority languages who take advantage of opportunities to be educated through minority languages.

Languages, politics and education

In order to appreciate the situation of different language minorities today, it is important to understand political and historical developments. Colonialism, imperialism, nationalism and globalization are complex and sometimes overlapping policies with important consequences for the education of minorities. The associated practices underline the power relations between dominant and minority groups.

Colonialism

Colonialism involves the extension of territorial control by a stronger power over a weaker people (Nardo, 2006). The most active practitioners were Europeans who, between the 15th and the 20th centuries, sent settlers to populate all of North and South America, Australia, and Aotearoa/New Zealand. Colonists and the diseases they brought with them were responsible for the deaths of very large numbers of Indigenous peoples; warfare added to the toll. For instance, the Indigenous population of the US reduced from an estimated ten million in 1492 to less than 250,000 in 1900 (Thornton, 1987). Oppression is the hallmark of colonialism, as witnessed by atrocities such as the death of several thousand Cherokees on a forced march to 'Indian territory' in Oklahoma. Children were also removed from their parents. To take just one example, in Australia in the early 20th century, the 'stolen generations' of mixed race children were forcibly removed from their parents to special homes and foster families and stripped of all vestiges of their linguistic and cultural heritage (HREOC, 1992). Corporal punishment and verbal humiliation were also widely used.

The cumulative effects of centuries of oppression have inevitably taken their toll on Indigenous languages. Only 154 of an estimated 300 plus languages have survived in the United States; of these, only a tiny proportion are being passed on to children by their parents and elders in the traditional way (Francis & Reyhner, 2002). The situation in Canada is very similar (Statistics Canada, 1998). Only three of the 50 surviving Aboriginal languages now have large enough populations to be considered secure. In Australia, between 200 and 250 languages were spoken at the time of European settlement. Many were quickly lost as the local populations died or were displaced; those that survive are spoken mainly in the sparsely populated areas of central and northern Australia. According to the 2001 census, fewer than 50 of the original languages now survive.

Ironically, the education systems which initially played a key role in the oppression of Indigenous languages are now involved in attempts to reverse language shift as, for instance, in the case of Māori in Aotearoa/New Zealand (May *et al.*, 2006).

Case Study: Te reo Māori in Aotearoa/New Zealand

The most significant development in education of Maori children in Aotearoa/New Zealand was initiated by the Māori themselves. The priority of leaders was to reattach the language to the people at community level. Te kohanga reo, or language nests, were established by parents in the early 1980s and are staffed by Māori-speaking parents, grandparents and caregivers. The aim is to immerse pre-school children in the language, following a curriculum that validates Māori knowledge, learning styles and administrative practices.

Parents anxious to maintain the language gains made by their children in the language nests pressed first for Māori-medium primary schools and later Māori-medium secondary schools. By 2001, about 17% of Maori children were enrolled in some form of Māori-medium provision. The four main kinds of program are based on the proportion of Māori used in teaching: level 1 (between 81 and 100%); level 2 (between 51 and 80%); level 3 (between 31 and 50%) and level 4 (between 12 and 30 %).

The most effective programmes have proved to be those with the highest level of immersion in Māori (levels 1 and 2). In 2004, the proportion of Māori students attaining National Certificate of Educational Achievement (NCEA) in year 11 was higher in level 1 and 2 schools than in other schools; so, too, were the grades which they achieved. Reasons why this may be the case are discussed in Chapter 4 (see The Interdependence Hypothesis, p.59).

Imperialism

Imperialism, like colonialism, involves the control of one or a number of countries by a dominant nation. It is associated in particular with the 'scramble for Africa', during the late 19th century, as various European powers struggled to capture new overseas markets (Harlow & Carter, 2003; Rassool *et al.*, 2007). There are, however, important differences between the earlier and later exercise of power. Colonialism involves settlement by incomers who, over time, become the most numerous group; imperialism entails the control of foreign dependencies by relatively small numbers of incomers. In countries such as Australia, Aotearoa/New Zealand, Canada and the US, Indigenous peoples over time became the minority. In contrast, Africans, continue to form the majority.

Local languages were often used in the early days in missionary schools but were soon replaced by European languages (Edwards, 2004). The policy has had the effect of disenfranchising large sections of the population and relegating local languages to low status, oral usage. It also contributes to economic and social disparities: fluency in European languages is associated with 'being educated' and is therefore seen as a prerequisite for upward social mobility (Myers-Scotton, 1993). In discussing minority languages in an African context, the benchmark is, of course, the greater power associated with the European languages spoken by the dominant group rather than the numbers of speakers.

Most attempts to incorporate African languages in education in the years following Independence in the second half of the 20th century foundered in the face of inadequate resources and lack of political will. The educational consequences of insisting on the exclusive use of European languages are tragic, as illustrated by Kwasi Opoku-Amankwa's (2008) classroom observations in Ghana.

Case study: A stranger comes to school

In an English lesson in primary 4A, the teacher was going through the *Test yourself review exercises* in the textbook. Amakpor arrived ten minutes into the lesson and was reprimanded for his lateness before the teacher continued with the lesson.

Teacher:	Let's move on. What is the next word?
Pupils:	Theirs (pronounced like dears)
Teacher:	Not dears, it's theirs. When pronouncing, say *th*; the other one is *d*. Can anybody form a sentence?
Pupils:	These books is theirs
Teacher:	When you say *these books* you don't say *is*, you say *are*. Say it again.
Pupils:	These books are theirs
Teacher:	Any other example?
Pupils:	These pens are theirs These shoe are theirs
Teacher:	Shoe. One?

At this point, the teacher asks Amakpor to point to *hers* from a list of seven words on the board, including *theirs, mine, his* and *ours*. Amakpor is rooted to the spot. The teacher asks another pupil to show him the word. Amakpor still cannot spell the word. Determined to persist, she asks Amakpor to pick out *his* from some flashcards. Still no success, and Amakpor is not the only 'stranger' in the class. When the teacher turns her attention to Steve and Mike, it is evident that they, too, are mere spectators watching the teacher and a few 'good' pupils perform.

Teacher:	Form sentences with the word *hers*. Yes Steve...
Steve:	[fumbles] This is hers book
Teacher:	No... *hers*. Yes Mike...
Mike:	The ruler has hers.
Teacher:	You are just saying something for saying sake. I saw you playing, that is why I called you. Keep standing... let's move on to number five, OURS.

In the next question on 'changing positives to negatives', we see a similar pattern with many of the pupils unable to answer.

Teacher:	We are going to change sentences into negative forms... *Afi killed the snake* is in the positive form and we want to change it to negative form. So the answer is *Afi didn't kill the snake*. Here we change the past to what...? Present. The verb here should be what? Present because of the *didn't*. You should bring the present verb so the... okay let's go on. Number one. Yes Evans, read number one for us.
Evans:	Fati broke the glass
Teacher:	I have explained something here for you. I said when you bring *didn't* the verb should be present. So the verb is what? *Broke*. Then we change it to what? Present tense. Yes Vida? [Vida stands up but says nothing.] We're supposed to change the *broke* to what... present not past. We shouldn't

> use the past again, we should use the present word for *broke*. Yes Anane? [No response from Anane. Of the eleven pupils called on by the teacher, only four were able to give correct answers].
>
> Later on during break time, when I asked Amakopor in Twi why he was late, he replied: 'My father delayed me. I was waiting to collect money from him to pay off my examination printing fee but he said he had no money. I thought I would be driven out from class'. When I asked Amakopor why he failed to tell his teacher what he had just told me, he was frank: 'I couldn't say it in English. Madam would insist that I say it in English'.

The classroom interactions in this Ghanaian classroom illustrate the 'safetalk' that results when neither teachers nor children are fluent in the language of instruction (Chick, 1996). Interest in establishing African languages before the introduction of languages of wider communication is, however, growing. Long-standing prejudice about the suitability of African languages as vehicles of education is being challenged by academics, non-governmental organizations and official bodies such as African Academy of Languages (ACALAN), the language body of the African Union (ADEA *et al.*, 2005; Alexander, 2005).

Linguistic imperialism is not, of course, limited to Africa. The role of English as an instrument in the foreign policy of English-speaking countries is a central theme for writers such as Pennycook (1994) and Phillipson (2000).

Nationalism

The main linguistic casualties of nation-building in 19th century Europe (see chapter two) are the so-called 'lesser-used' languages (Edwards, 2004; Extra & Gorter, 2001). On some occasions, these languages are spoken within the boundaries of a single nation state, as is the case for Irish in Ireland. On other occasions, state borders cut through a single language area, as is the case for Catalan, spoken in parts of Spain, France, Italy and Andorra, or Basque in France and Spain. The same language can be a majority language in one setting and a minority language in others. Danish, for instance, is the official language of Denmark and a minority language in Germany.

As is the case for Indigenous languages, the fate of most lesser-used languages is inextricably linked with a particular territory: if it were no longer spoken in that location, it would disappear forever. Although many of the lesser-used languages have sustainable numbers of speakers for the present at least, others are unlikely to be transmitted to the next generation. Ladin, a language spoken in the Dolomite Mountains in Italy, for instance, has an estimated 30,000 speakers, while Wendisch, a Western Slavonic language spoken in the region of Lower Lusatia, is now spoken only by the older generation.

Some of the issues for educators working with lesser-used languages are illustrated by the case study of Basque.

Case study: Basque in Euskara

Basque is spoken in the Pyrenees of north-central Spain and the adjoining region of southwest France. Of the 1 million speakers, some 700,000 use Basque as a first language. Like other lesser-used languages in Europe, Basque has been the target for extremely oppressive government policies. In the early 20th century, for instance, the use of Basque was banned in public. It was only following the death of General Franco in 1979 when considerable autonomy was gained from central government, that ikastolak – or Basque immersion schools – began appearing.

The proportion of minority language speakers varies from one location to the next, as does support for the use of Basque in education. It is impractical, then, to impose a one-size-fits-all solution. Today, schooling takes three main forms (Mercator Education, undated):

- Type A schools attended by 8.1% of students where education is entirely in Spanish, but Basque is studied as a compulsory subject.
- Type B schools attended by 30.5% of students where both Basque and Spanish are used as the medium of instruction.
- Type D (there is no letter C in Basque) schools attended by 61.4 per cent of students where education is entirely in Basque and Spanish is studied as a compulsory subject.

Provision in the Northern Basque country is much more limited. The first Ikastola was opened by parents in 1964. By 2007, some 25 Ikastolak were serving over 2000 children from the ages of two to 18. The aim of the Ikastolak is to provide an immersion experience which will ensure that even children from non-Basque-speaking backgrounds are proficient in both spoken and written Basque by the end of primary school. French is taught as a subject at primary level; at the secondary level, the same amount of time is spent on French language and literature as in mainstream schools.

A federation of Ikastolak offers opportunities for collaboration throughout the Basque region on special education projects, cultural events and continuing professional development for teachers. Northern Ikastolak also have links with a national organization of language minority educators bringing them together with Breton, Occitan, Catalan and Alsatian schools.

Globalization

Globalization, like the other policies we have been discussing, resists any single or simple definition, but is generally held to refer to economic integration on a global scale (Lechner & Boli, 2004). This process dates back to the Silk Road, which connected China and the Mediterranean in ancient times. It was also evident in the 17th century with the operation of the Dutch East India Company, sometimes dubbed the first multinational corporation, and the colonial and imperial adventurism of the centuries that followed (Wild, 2000). In recent years the pace of globalization has, however, accelerated with challenges to the supremacy of nation states from supranational developments, including cross-border flows of investments, services and ideas.

There is a similar transnational flow of languages (Edwards, 2004). In the 2001 Canadian census, one in every six people reported a home language other than English or French; more than 100 different languages were recorded. The 2001 Australian census reported that 142 languages, in addition to Aboriginal languages, were spoken by just over one in six of the population. According to the 2000 US census, the proportion of people speaking a home language other than English was even higher: one in five. In the UK, over 300 different languages were recorded in the most recent survey of London schoolchildren (Baker & Eversley, 2000).

Unlike Indigenous and lesser-used languages, language death is not an issue for these 'new minorities': if Chinese were no longer used in San Francisco or Sydney, there would be no shortage of Chinese speakers elsewhere. Language maintenance is, however, an extremely important concern for communication within the family and cultural identities; and, as we saw in Chapter 2, linguistic diversity has advantages for both individuals and the wider society.

So how have educationalists responded to the 'superdiversity' that defines the late 20th and 21st centuries? Policies have varied considerably across time and space, as illustrated by the overviews which follow of developments in the UK, the US and Australia in the second half of the 20th century. The final case study concerns international schools, another symptom of globalization. Originally established to serve expatriate English speakers, non-native speakers now constitute over half the students in these schools.

Case study: The UK

Policy and practice In the 1950s and 1960s, when children speaking languages other than English began arriving in large numbers in British schools, was laissez-faire. The unquestioned assumption was that children would 'pick up English in the playground' and that the language of the home had no place in schools (Edwards, 2004).

The first acknowledgement of bilingualism as a resource for learning came in 1975 with the publication of the Bullock Report, *A Language for Life,* which made an impassioned plea for schools to respect the cultural and linguistic diversity of their students: 'No child should be expected to cast off the language and culture of the home as he crosses the school threshold and the curriculum should reflect those aspects of his life'. Bilingualism was presented as an asset to be nurtured and schools were encouraged to 'help maintain and deepen... knowledge of the mother tongues'.

UK attitudes towards bilingualism are inconsistent. Official support is given for education through the medium of Welsh in Wales, Gaelic in Scotland and Irish in Ireland. The possibility of extending bilingual education to other languages, however, received a body blow with the publication in 1985 of the Swann Report, *Education for All,* which recommended that there should be no separate provision to help children maintain their family languages. In the belief that attempts to promote minority languages in the mainstream would be divisive, the main responsibility was placed on ethnic minority communities themselves. There were two exceptions to this broad English-only policy. The first was that, where practicable, children should be provided with 'bilingual support' – classroom assistants or teachers able to speak to them in their own language and help them make the transition from home to school; the second was the inclusion of non-traditional languages in the language curriculum of secondary schools where there was sufficient demand.

The publication of the National Languages Strategy in 2002 marked a shift towards more inclusive attitudes towards new minority languages. Until this point, modern language teaching was limited to European languages; for the first time, the importance of selected new minority languages, including Arabic, Chinese and Panjabi was acknowledged.

Case study: Australia

In Australia, events took a rather different course. Concern for social equity was reinforced by the quest for a new national identity. As ties with Britain gradually loosened, a new policy of 'unity in diversity' challenged traditional notions of nationality. The debate was broadened from the language learning needs of individuals to multicultural education for all Australians. The 1976 report of the Committee on the Teaching of Migrant Languages in School, for instance, recommended not only that schools should meet the continuing needs of migrant children to learn their own languages but that all children should have the opportunity to acquire an understanding of other languages from the earliest years of primary school.

As was the case in the UK, there was a policy shift in the 1980s from specialist provision to the mainstreaming of provision for English as a Second Language. While there has been greater emphasis on the professionalization of ESL teachers and the raising of awareness of content (or subject) for teachers of the needs of second language learners, there remains a tendency to view what Davison (2001) terms 'ESL-ness' as a problem rather than a resource.

Ongoing activism on the part of ethnic minority communities, linguists and other intellectuals led ultimately to the groundbreaking National Policy on Languages in 1990. The policy was based on four main principles: availability of English and English literacy for all; support for Aboriginal and Torres Straits Islander languages; a language other than English for all; and access for all to equitable language services. One of its more notable achievements was the way in which other languages were presented as complementary – and not subordinated – to English.

Subsequent fine-tuning to the policy had the effect of reducing the impact of the original manifesto. The title of the White Paper, *The Australian Language and Literacy Policy* (Australia, 1991) gave important clues about new priorities, with the change from *languages* to *language* and the addition of *literacy*. Although many of the original commitments remained, the notion of the nation's languages as an important cultural resource was considerably underplayed.

Case study: The US

From the early 1960s, teachers were actively exploring alternative solutions to the problems faced by non-English-speaking children in the US, including bilingual education. Middle-class Cuban refugees in Dade County, Florida were among the first to demand changes in their children's education (Crawford, 1999). The first experimental bilingual program was opened to Spanish- and English-speaking students at the Coral Way Elementary School in 1963 where students achieved the same level or higher than their counterparts in mainstream schools. The success of Coral Way led to similar programs across the country.

The enthusiasm of educators soon attracted political support. The Bilingual Education Act was passed in 1968; in 1970 a memorandum was issued requiring school districts with at least a 5% minority student population to comply with the law. While some districts took the necessary steps, others did nothing. It rapidly became clear that something stronger than a memorandum would be necessary to ensure compliance.

Edward Steinman, a poverty lawyer in San Francisco, first discovered the problems faced by Chinese children when Kam Wai Lau came to him with a work complaint (Del Valle, 2003). Her six-year-old son, Kinney, was one of at least 1800 Chinese-speaking children who were receiving no language support in school; he became head plaintiff in a class action suit on behalf of Chinese heritage students filed against the San Francisco Unified School District, which argued that the students were disadvantaged because they could not understand the language of instruction. After a series of defeats in lower courts, the Supreme Court finally sided with Lau in 1974.

Procedures to be followed by school boards were first outlined in the so-called Lau Remedies and later spelled out in official regulations published by the Office of Civil Rights. Students dominant in a language other than English were to be placed in bilingual programs; English-dominant students could be placed in English-only programs; students with equal proficiency in two languages could choose either an English-only or a bilingual program. Compliance with the Lau decision, however, remained patchy (Crawford, 1999).

Shortages of trained teachers and teaching materials meant that bilingual education programs remained an option for only a relatively small proportion of students. Two main kinds of program were offered – early exit and late exit. Early-exit – or transitional – bilingual programs provide initial instruction in the children's first language in the early stages of learning to read and for purposes of clarification. First language instruction is phased out rapidly, so that most students are in mainstream classes by the end of the first or second grade. In late-exit programs, which continue throughout elementary school, students receive part of their instruction in their first language, even when they have achieved fluency in English. Early-exit programs tend to view children's home languages as a problem to be solved and have a remedial orientation. In contrast, late-exist models consider home languages a resource and are enrichment orientated.

While public opinion was relatively content to support transitional bilingual programs, there was considerable opposition to maintenance programs. The reauthorizations of the Bilingual Education Act in the 1980s began to give greater prominence to English language programs, as political pressure against bilingual education grew. Faced with the growing erosion of support, pro-bilingual education senators ordered a study (US General Accounting Office, 1987) which reported that bilingual education programs *were* effective. In a compromise move, Congress stopped short of bringing bilingual education programs to an end but agreed that English-only programs would qualify for the same federal funds.

Negative media coverage made it very difficult for advocates of bilingual education to make their case (McQuillan & Tse, 1996). Journalists have clearly been influenced by expensive anti-bilingual education campaigns funded by figures such as Ron Unz, using his personal fortune. In 1998, California voters approved Proposition 227, an initiative that largely eliminated bilingual education from the state's public schools. Arizona followed with Proposition 203, a similar measure, in 2000. Unz also funded an unsuccessful campaign for an amendment to the Colorado constitution.

After 34 years of controversy, the Bilingual Education Act was finally replaced in 2002 by Title 111 of No Child Left Behind (NCLB), in which the sole emphasis is on the rapid acquisition of English. The intention was to establish 'measurable achievement objectives', and to punish failure to show progress in annual English assessments. Early indications are that NCLB is delivering no measurable improvements in educational outcomes for bilingual students and is causing great unhappiness among educators. Many of the criticisms center on the disproportionate amounts of time spent 'teaching to the test' and the consequent narrowing of the curriculum. The focus on testing also detracts attention from other obstacles to achievement, such as suitably trained teachers, unequal access to resources and poorly designed instructional programs (Crawford, 2005; 2008; Wright, 2005).

Case study: International schools

The first international schools date back to the post-Second World War period and were set up to serve the children of the large numbers of English-speaking diplomats, business men and others sent abroad to work on a temporary basis (Carder, 2007). Over the years, however, they have accepted growing numbers of students from the countries where they are based, as well as the children of expatriates from non-English-speaking countries. Currently the majority of students are non-native speakers of English. The exclusive medium of instruction in by far the largest proportion of international schools is English. As is the case for English-speaking parents who enroll their children in French immersion or Spanish–English dual language programs, the aim is to benefit from the economic and social advantages of bilingualism. For students in international schools, however, the target language is English, the new global lingua franca.

There are clearly differences between the situation of non-native speakers of English in international schools and speakers of new minority languages in national systems. There is no question, for instance, of assimilating sojourners who need to maintain their home languages for their return. Both groups of students, however, find themselves at a disadvantage when their first languages are excluded. For this reason, there is a growing movement within international schools for the tripartite model proposed by Carder (2007), comprising an ESL program taught in parallel to the mainstream; a program of language and content awareness for mainstream teachers; and a mother tongue program.

Greater flexibility in accreditation will make it possible to achieve this end. The International Baccalaureate Diploma, recognized as a qualification for university entrance in many countries, requires students to study six subjects including a first and second language. Assessment regularly takes place in 44 first languages and another 34 languages by special request. While many non-native English-speaking students fail to reach the level required for English as a first language, they are now able to write examinations in their mother tongues, with English (or another language) as their second language. In the region of 35% of students at the Vienna International School, for instance, opt for this solution. Teachers report that literacy in both languages is improving, as are grades in all their subjects.

Limitations of reliance on education

Education, then, has formed the main line of defense in attempts to slow, or even reverse language shift in the case of both Indigenous and lesser-used languages. Not all language shift theorists, however, are convinced that education is the panacea that it might seem at first sight. Fishman (1991), in particular, argues that, while education plays an important role, it cannot assume sole responsibility for reversing language shift.

There is growing awareness of the problems associated with over-reliance on education (Edwards, 2004). The Irish experience is a case in point. Education was seen as the main tool in language revival with the emergence of the Free State in 1921. Given the level of official support, the gains were disappointing. According to the 2002 census, 42.8% of the population of the Republic speak Irish, but two-thirds of these reported that they never used the language or used it less than once a week. If the minority language is not to be associated primarily with the classroom, authentic social spaces need to be created for its use.

The challenge for language planners in Europe, then, is to persuade parents of the benefits of transmitting the language to their children. The challenge for language activists in Africa, in contrast, is to persuade parents of the benefits of bilingual education.

In all settings, the main obstacles to progress are the widespread negative attitudes towards the languages of less powerful peoples. Bourdieu (1991, 1997) explains this negativity in terms of méconnaissance (or misrecognition) whereby the politically dominant persuade subordinated groups that their language and culture are inferior; he talks of the symbolic violence inflicted when such attempts succeed.

But Bourdieu (1991: 66–67) also points to a possible way out of this impasse. His analysis of language and power draws heavily on metaphors from economics. He talks, for instance, about 'linguistic products ... signs of wealth or capital, which receive their value only in relation to a market, characterized by a particular law of price formation'. In this analysis language marketing is a potential tool for counteracting widespread myths about minority languages. The two case studies which follow illustrate the potential role of language marketing in achieving more equitable education outcomes.

Case study: Promoting minority languages in Wales

The Twf ('Growth') project was launched in March 2002 to promote the benefits of bilingualism to parents (Edwards & Pritchard Newcombe, 2005). The core work of the project is with health professionals. Midwives are solely responsible for the care of all normal pregnancies and labors. Their contact with parents before the baby's birth means that they are ideally placed to discuss language choice. Two key questions included in patient-held records of pregnancy – *Which language/s do you intend introducing to your baby?* and *Have you received information about bilingualism from your midwife* – serve as a reminder to raise the issue at an early stage.

The work of health visitors, who take over from midwives soon after birth, is even more relevant: child development is central to their interests and language development is a topic which parents are often keen to discuss. Language issues are routinely raised at the eight-month assessment and at other points as the opportunity arises.

Midwives and health visitors have access to families at times critical for influencing decisions about language. Most important, they are respected and enjoy a relationship of trust with parents. As a result, their involvement in the work of the project is likely to have a positive effect on perceptions of the Twf message. But at the same time, it is important to recognize that Twf is in competition with many other demands on health professionals' time and that commitment to promoting bilingualism is also influenced by personal experiences – both positive and negative – with the Welsh language.

Twf workers also cooperate with other organizations. They distribute information through signposting organizations such as the Children's Information Bureau and libraries. They give presentations to childbirth preparation classes and a wide range of preschool groups. They also work with other Welsh language organizations in staging events to promote the language.

The project has developed a range of marketing materials likely to appeal to the widest possible audience. The leaflet, *6 good reasons for making sure your children can speak Welsh* (Figure 3.1) neatly encapsulates the Twf message about the benefits of bilingualism. The leaflet is included in women's Record of Pregnancy and in the 'Bounty pack' of free samples and advertising literature distributed to every woman giving birth in hospitals in Wales.

Er mwyn y plant

6 rheswm da dros roi cyfle i'ch plant ddysgu Cymraeg.
Dwy iaith - dwy waith y dewis.
Gall siarad dwy iaith roi eich plentyn ar y blaen.

For the sake of your children

6 good reasons for giving your children the chance to speak Welsh.
Two languages - twice the choice.
Speaking two languages can give your children a head start.

Yn yr ysgol

Mae plant sy'n dysgu dwy iaith ar y blaen wrth ddarllen a chyfri. Maen nhw'n aml yn gwneud yn well mewn arholiadau yn nes ymlaen.

At school

Children who learn two languages have a head start when reading and counting. They often do better in exams later on.

❷

Yn y teulu

Mae dysgu dwy iaith yn haws i blant bach. O fewn dim, byddan nhw'n symud yn hwylus o un i'r llall. Fe fydd yr holl deulu wrth eu bodd.

In the family

Learning two languages is easier for young children. In no time at all they'll be switching easily from one to the other. The whole family will be proud.

❹

Yn y gwaith

Mae dwy iaith yn rhoi gwell dewis ym myd gwaith. Mae llawer o swyddi yng Nghymru angen sgiliau Cymraeg a Saesneg.

At work

Two languages offer a better choice of work. Many employers in Wales ask for Welsh and English skills.

❻

Yn y gymdeithas

Mae'n deimlad braf gallu symud yn hawdd o un iaith i'r llall. Fe fydd siarad y ddwy iaith yn agor y drws i wneud ffrindiau newydd.

In the community

It gives you a buzz to be able to switch easily from one language to another. Speaking both languages opens doors to make new friends.

⑧

Yn y byd

Mae'r rhan fwya o bobl y byd yn gallu siarad mwy nag un iaith. Ar ôl dysgu'r ail, mae'n haws dysgu rhagor wedyn. Mae Cymraeg yn rhoi dechrau da.

Around the world

Most people throughout the world can speak more than one language. After learning two, it's much easier to learn more. Welsh gives you a good start.

⑩

Mewn bywyd

Mae Saesneg a Chymraeg yn gyfoethog iawn, yn llawn straeon a chaneuon, hanes a hwyl. Fe fydd eich plentyn yn cael y gorau o'r ddau fyd.

In life

Both English and Welsh are like treasure troves, full of stories and songs, history and fun. Your child will have the best of both worlds.

⑫

Figure 3.1 *6 good reasons for making sure your children can speak Welsh* leaflet, available from: www.byig-wlb.org.uk.

> **Case study:** Advocacy for African languages in South Africa
>
> The South African Constitution recognizes 11 official languages (nine African languages, English and Afrikaans) as part of an attempt to reinstate previously subjugated languages. Each province chooses its own official languages suited to its population groupings, and each school governing body has the power to determine its own language policy. The success of this human rights approach will depend to a significant extent on the availability of adequately skilled language teachers and appropriate teaching resources. It will also depend on a significant shift in language attitudes.
>
> Kamwangamalu (2001) argues for a market-oriented approach to mother tongue education. First and foremost, language consumers need to be persuaded that the use of an African language as a medium of instruction will lead to greater job opportunities and upward social mobility. There is a palpable tension between the perception of parents, on the one hand, that the surest route to upward mobility is through English-medium education and the firm belief of policymakers, on the other hand, that a strong foundation in the children's mother tongue will lead to more equitable outcomes. The situation is further complicated by historical considerations. During the apartheid era, Africans were denied access to English in education; efforts to promote African languages therefore give rise to considerable suspicion.
>
> While the rate of change is disappointingly slow, there are signs of progress. The Western Cape is a case in point. As part of the process of implementing a policy of bilingual education for children in the first six years of schooling, the Education Department understands the need to challenge long-standing myths about the assumed superiority of English and has launched a language advocacy program aimed at education department officials, teachers and parents. Initial responses to this initiative have been mixed, with very clearly discernible resistance on the part of many people. Given the distance to be covered in a society where racist apartheid policies are still recent history, these language advocacy efforts nonetheless represent an important start.

Marginalized languages

Non-standard languages and sign languages have much in common with other minority languages. They, too, have been excluded from formal schooling, often with unfortunate consequences. Children who speak non-standard forms of English are sometimes dismissed as stupid or lazy although such judgments are often couched in more politically correct terms such as 'disadvantaged' or 'language deficient' (Edwards, 2004). The situation of sign languages is more problematic still. Here the issue was not whether these varieties were substandard, but whether they were languages at all.

It is only since the 1960s that linguists and educators have acknowledged that varieties such as those spoken by African–Caribbeans in the UK, African–Americans in the US and Aboriginals in Australia are valid, rule-governed language systems. Sign languages had to wait another 20 years before they received similar recognition (Ladd, 2003). The carefully marshalled evidence of linguists, however, has exerted relatively little influence on education policy. While lip service has been paid to the role of non-standard varieties in many children's language repertoire, opportunities for using non-standard language in classrooms remain limited; black and working-class children are left in little doubt as to the low status of the language they bring with them to the classroom.

Case study: African-American Vernacular in US education

African-American Vernacular (also known as Black English and Ebonics) in education was the subject of a legal challenge in 1979 in the case of Martin Luther King Jr Elementary School v. Ann Arbor School District (Labov, 1982). African Americans were over-represented in the number of suspensions and under-represented in honors classes in this affluent, college town in the Midwest. Two-thirds of the plaintiff children in the class action had been classified as having special educational needs.

The court accepted expert testimony that, by looking at Black English Vernacular as a series of mistakes, teachers were failing to understand its logic and its structures. Although Black English was not found to be an obstacle in itself, it was judged that teacher insensitivity could pose a barrier to learning to read and use standard English. The ruling did not require the school board to teach children in or through Black English, but simply to help its teachers to recognize the home language of the students and to use that knowledge in teaching reading skills.

Nearly 20 years later, the circumstances surrounding the resolution passed by the Oakland Unified School District Board of Education in California bore a striking resemblance to the Ann Arbor case (Perry & Delpit, 1997). The school board members, community activists and teachers that made up its African-American task force were faced with alarming discrepancies between the attainment of African–American and other students. Other indicators were also cause for concern: African-Americans, who made up 53% of the student population, represented 80 per cent of suspensions and 71% of students with special educational needs.

Members of the task force were, however, struck by the above-average performance of African-American students at Prescott Elementary School, the only school in the Oakland school district where most teachers were participating in the Standard English Proficiency program (SEP), a state-wide initiative in which Black English was used to help children learn to read and write in standard English. In December 1996, the board unanimously passed the Ebonics Resolution, which required all schools in the district to take part in the SEP program as part of a broad strategy aimed at improving the school performance of African-American students.

The intensity of response to the Oakland resolution was unprecedented. The media, in the form of editorial writers, columnists and talk-show hosts, were almost universally hostile. It was widely – and inaccurately – reported that Oakland students would be taught Ebonics instead of standard English; rebuttals from spokespeople for the board were ignored.

Linguists and educators united in an attempt to provide an informed perspective on the confused public debate. The efforts of professionals, sadly, were to limited effect: the furore over the Oakland resolution goes well beyond linguistics. It is a debate about culture, power, identity and control. Minority students are only too aware that, even if they use the majority dialect, they will not automatically be accepted into the mainstream.

Case study: Sign languages

Oralism – the exclusive approach to Deaf education for the best part of a century – banned sign languages from the classroom. Awareness of the devastating effects of this policy, however, is relatively recent. A survey of all UK Deaf school leavers (Conrad, 1979) revealed that 16-year-olds had an average reading age of less than nine years and much of their spoken English was unintelligible; their lip-reading skills were no better than those of hearing people trying to lip read for the first time. Similar findings have been reported in the US (Bowe, 1991; Wolk & Schildroth, 1986).

The mid-1970s saw the introduction of a compromise measure, an approach known as Total Communication, which involves the simultaneous use of sign and speech. The sign in question, however, was an artificial system, specially devised to follow English grammar. The results were disappointing. Although the intention was to help children acquire spoken English, differences in modality – sound versus vision – mean that Signed English is often difficult to follow for children accustomed to natural sign languages. The use of Signed English to teach spoken English to Deaf children is thus akin to using French to teach German to Spanish students.

As recognition of the various natural sign languages has grown, so, too, have calls for bilingual education and, over the last decade, considerable progress has been made in developing bilingual policies and pedagogies (Ladd, 2003; Swanwick & Gregory, 2007). During this time, the Deaf community has also grown in political awareness and self-confidence. While most hearing people continue to perceive deafness as a disability, many Deaf people contest this view, arguing that they are rather members of a cultural and linguistic minority.

Minority languages and majority speakers

Many discussions of multilingualism in education focus exclusively on the needs of minority language speakers and fail to recognize that benefits also accrue to speakers of majority languages. There are two main examples where the speakers of the dominant language make a deliberate decision to educate their children bilingually: immersion programs and two-way bilingual programs.

Immersion programs

Immersion programs where, in the initial stages at least, the minority language is used as the main or exclusive medium of instruction are now in common use for a range of Indigenous and lesser-used languages. They were first developed, however, to serve the needs of majority language speakers. Canada has been the leader in this field with in excess of 300,000 students enrolled in immersion programs. Foreign language immersion programs have also gained ground in the US and Australia. Parents persuaded that 'bilingual is beautiful' want to capitalize on the advantages associated with a knowledge of other languages. The aim here, then, is additive bilingualism.

Case study: French immersion

In the mid-1960s, the Anglophone minority community in Quebec realized that proficiency in French would soon be a prerequisite for economic survival (Baker & Prys Jones, 1998). It was equally apparent that the diet of grammar, translation and drills experienced by previous generations had been a poor preparation either for work or for socialization in French.

In 1965, a small group of English-speaking parents in St Lambert, a suburb of Montreal, started to explore possible alternatives in discussion with scholars in bilingualism at McGill University. In the model they proposed, English-speaking children would be immersed in French for the first years of schooling; English would then be introduced gradually until, by Grade 6, half the curriculum would be in English and half in French. Initial attempts at lobbying for immersion schooling were unsuccessful but support for the initiative from the local press and the persistence of parents eventually persuaded the school board to relent. Financial support was provided by the 1970 Official Languages in Education Program.

Interest across the country was fanned by media stories about immersion education in Quebec. Another factor in the popularity of French immersion was the intense interest of researchers and the widespread dissemination of their results. The findings from research in Canada (and subsequently in many other countries) show consistently that immersion students acquire normal English proficiency, as well as a high level in the second language; critically, they show the same or better achievement as children in mainstream schools. Data collected for the 2000 Programme for International Student Assessment (PISA) are also consistent with this pattern: students in French immersion programs performed significantly better in reading than non-immersion students (Allen, 2004).

As immersion education has spread to other settings, a number of variations have emerged. Distinctions are now made between total immersion where all the subjects in the lower grades (K–2) are taught in the second language and instruction in English increases in the upper grades (3–6) to 20–50%. In partial immersion programs, up to half the subjects are taught in the second language; sometimes the material taught in the second language is reinforced in English. There is also variation in the stage at which the second language is introduced. Mid-immersion programs start in Grades 4 or 5 and late immersion programs in Grades 6 or 7.

Two-way bilingual programs

Two-way bilingual education involves a balance of language-minority and language-majority students, where each group makes up between one-third and two-thirds of the total student population and the non-English language is used at least half of the time (Howard & Sugarman, 2007; Prez, 2003). Interest in this model is probably due to the convergence of bilingual education research, which suggests that native language development has positive educational outcomes for language-minority students, and foreign language immersion research, which demonstrates the benefits for native English speakers.

Jessica's parents chose a dual language program because they wanted their daughter to be bilingual. In the case study which follows, based on Lindholm-Leary (2000), we look at what it feels like as an English speaker in the early days in a classroom where the teacher uses English for approximately 20 minutes every day and the rest of the time interactions are in Spanish.

Case study: Day 5 in a Spanish-English kindergarten

Jessica walks into class, hearing English and Spanish spoken all around her by her classmates. She looks on the wall and sees many colourful displays. Like most children of her age, she doesn't read yet although she may recognize some words. An English-speaking classmate greets her enthusiastically in English. The teacher calls the class to order in Spanish, makes eye contact with her students and beckons them to come up front and sit on the carpet. She says and gesticulates to sit down. On Monday when the teacher told the children 'Venga a la alfombra', Jessica may have been puzzled. One or two of the children may have eagerly translated for her, or she may have just looked around and followed the teacher to the front. But now Jessica and her friends have probably already learned this classroom routine and know what the teacher wants.

Ms Sánchez is going through the calendar activities in Spanish. She uses pictures, objects, gestures and carefully enunciated speech to help the English-speaking children understand. Since Jessica has a calendar at home and this is now a familiar activity, she joins in reciting the days of the week. It doesn't matter if she forgets because there are always some students who know all the days. Then they count the days ... uno, duo, tres and so on. After a few days, Jessica remembers these words.

Later that day, Jessica is in a math group. Ms Sánchez shows the children how to group beads into two piles – grande and pequeño. Jessica notices that the teacher puts one red bead in the grande pile and another in the pequeño pile. Hmmm... Then she notices that the teacher is putting the little beads into the pequeño pile and the big beads in the grande pile. Excitedly she picks up a bead, says, 'Grande' and puts it in the grande pile. 'Maestra, look I did it, I know "grande"'. Mrs Sánchez replies with, 'Si muy bien, Jessica'. Jessica can tell by her eyes and tone of voice that she did a good job.

Key points

Language, politics and education

This chapter has looked at educational responses to multilingualism through the lens of four historical policies and practices – colonialism, imperialism, nationalism and globalization – each of which raises a range of issues for the education of minorities

- In **colonialism** incomers, over time, become the most numerous group and Indigenous peoples form the minority. The main concern is to ensure the survival of their languages in the face of rapidly declining numbers. Where parents are no longer able to transmit languages in the traditional way, the only hope of survival lies in immersion schooling which is also consistent with cultural values.

- **Imperialism** is particularly associated with the European control of African countries. Here foreign dependencies are controlled by relatively small numbers of incomers and speakers of local languages remain in the majority. However, the use of an unfamiliar European language as the medium of instruction disenfranchises large sections of the population and relegates local languages to low status, oral usage. The challenge here, then, is to incorporate local languages in education systems alongside languages of wider communication.

- The main casualties of 19th century European **nation-building** were lesser-used languages, such as Basque, Welsh and Frisian. As is the case for Indigenous languages, the main concern is to ensure the survival of their languages in the face of rapidly declining numbers.

- The unprecedented population movement associated with **globalization** in recent decades has given rise to a superdiversity of languages. Although language death is not an issue for speakers of these 'new minority' languages, speakers of new minority languages are none-the-less concerned with language transmission in order to ensure effective communication within the family and access to their cultural heritage.

While education has historically played a key role in the weakening minority languages, in more recent times it has often been important in reversing language shift through immersion programs. It is unwise, however, to place too much reliance on schooling. Parents need to be persuaded of the benefits of transmitting the language to their children and authentic social spaces need to be created for them to use minority languages.

Different national education systems have responded to the educational needs of new minority speakers in different ways. Most children depend on community support for their language learning; mainstream educators tend to either ignore their languages or regard them as a temporary crutch as they acquire English. Only in a relatively small proportion of cases do other languages play a meaningful role in instruction. Changing political priorities have had devastating effects on a wide range of programs and inadequate funding continues to be a major obstacle to progress.

There are clearly differences between the situation of non-native speakers of English, who now form the majority in international schools, and speakers of new minority languages in national systems. Both groups of students, however, find themselves at a disadvantage when their first languages are excluded from the classroom.

Marginalized languages

The speakers of marginalized languages such as non-standard dialects, creoles and sign languages have been particularly badly treated in education. There has been some movement, however, towards greater recognition of these contested varieties as valid linguistic systems in their own right.

Majority speakers and minority languages

In spite of ongoing opposition, support for other languages is much stronger than at any point in the recent past, as demonstrated by the growth in immersion and dual language programs for children from English-speaking families.

Activities and discussion points

1. What has been your experience of language learning in school? What have been the strengths and weaknesses of your exposure to other languages?

2. What kind of media coverage has there been in recent times of topics related to language and education where you live?

3. Use a database such as the one on the Council of International Schools website (http://members.cois.org/directory/isd.aspx) or the Directory of Two Way Immersion programs (www.cal.org/jsp/TWI/SchoolSearch.jsp) to locate two schools where it is possible to study in and through two languages. Then use the school website to collect information on the history of the programs and how they are currently organized. Compare and contrast provision.

4. Schools are busy places but, if you have access to a bilingual program as a former student or through a current member of staff, organize a visit and choose a class to observe. What do you notice about the patterns of language use and the children's responses? Check your observations out with students and with teachers.

Further reading

Indigenous education

Aboriginal links:
www.ammsa.com/ammsalinks.html
The North American links page of the
Aboriginal Multi-media Society.
Aboriginal education:
www.natsiew.nexus.edu.au
The Australian national website for
Aboriginal and Torres Strait Islanders.
Māori Education: www.minedu.govt.nz/
index.cfm?layout=index&indexid=1063
Information on some of the policy and
programs most relevant to Māori
learners.

Language and education in Africa

ADEA/ GTZ/Commonwealth Secretariat/
UIE (2005) *Optimizing Learning and
Education in Africa – the Language Factor.
A Stock-taking Research on Mother Tongue
and Bilingual Education in Sub-Saharan
Africa*. Retrieved from: www.adeanet.org/
biennial2006/doc/document/B3_1_
MTBLE_en.pdf
Brock-Utne, B. & Hopson, R. (2005)
*Languages of Instruction for African
Emancipation: Focus on Postcolonial
Contexts and Considerations*. African
Collective Books. Ann Arbor, MI:
Michigan State University Press.

The 'lesser-used' languages of Europe

Edwards, V. & Pritchard Newcombe (2005)
When School Is Not Enough.
*International Journal of Bilingualism and
Bilingual Education* 8(4): 298–312.
Cenoz, J. (ed.)(2008) *Teaching Through
Basque: Achievements and Challenges*.
Clevedon: Multilingual Matters.

European Bureau for Lesser-Used
Languages: www.eblul.org
An NGO promoting languages and
linguistic diversity in Europe.
Mercator-Education:
www.mercator-education.org
European network for information,
documentation and research into
regional or minority languages in
education.

Black language

Ramirez, D., Wiley, T., de Klerk, G. & Lee,
E. (2005) *Ebonics: The Urban Education
Debate* (2nd ed). Clevedon: Multilingual
Matters.
Alim, H.S. & Baugh, S. (eds) (2006) *Talkin
Black Talk: Language, Education, and
Social Change*. NY: Teachers College
Press.

Sign language

Ladd, P. (2003) *Understanding Deaf Culture:
In Search of Deafhood*. Clevedon:
Multilingual Matters
Swanwick, R. & Gregory, S. (2007) *Sign
Bilingual Education: Policy and Practice*.
Coleford, UK: Forest Books.

Bilingual education

Baker, C. (2006) *Foundations of Bilingualism
and Bilingual Education*. Clevedon:
Multilingual Matters.
de Courcy, M. (2002) *Learners' Experiences of
Immersion Education: Case Studies of
French and Chinese*. Clevedon:
Multilingual Matters.

Fortune, T.W. & Tedick, D. (eds) (2008) *Pathways to Multilingualism: Evolving Perspectives on Immersion Education.* Clevedon: Multilingual Matters.

May, S., Hill, R. & Tiakiwai, S. (2006) *Bilingual/Immersion Education: Indicators of Good Practice.* Wellington: Ministry of Education. Retrieved from: www.minedu.govt.nz/index.cfm?layout=document&documentid=11556&data=l#P2525_282054.

Potowski, K. (2007) *Language and Identity in a Dual Immersion School.* Clevedon: Multilingual Matters.

International schools

Carder, M. (2007) *Bilingualism in International Schools: A Model for Enriching Language Education.* Clevedon: Multilingual Matters.

Gallagher, E. (2008) *Equal Rights to the Curriculum. Many Languages, One Message.* Clevedon: Multilingual Matters.

English as a second language

Mohan, B., Leung, C. & Davison, C. (eds) (2001) *English as a Second Language in the mainstream: Teaching Learning and Identity.* Harlow, Longman Pearson.

4

4

Multiliteracies

In this chapter we look at literacy, an issue of central concern for educators working in multilingual classrooms, by asking the following key questions.

■ What is literacy? We introduce the different models developed to explain our interactions with the written word.

■ What are the issues for literacy in more than one language? We use the notion of continua of biliteracy to explore this highly complex phenomenon.

■ How is biliteracy best developed? Using key concepts developed by Jim Cummins we look at the conditions which are most likely to achieve success in a range of different settings.

What is literacy?

Chapter 2 addressed the question: what is a language? This chapter begins with an equally basic but very important question: what is literacy? The many different answers to this question across the years suggest that this is by no means a simple matter. At one time, being literate meant the ability to sign your name. Later definitions include reading or writing a simple sentence; describing your daily activities; self-reports of being able to read and write; and passing a written test of reading comprehension at a level comparable to an average student at Grade 4.

Traditionally, there has been a strong emphasis on the technical skills required for reading and writing, such as letter formation, spelling patterns and word recognition. In what is sometimes called the *autonomous model* of literacy (Street, 1997), these technical skills are considered part of a 'neutral' cognitive process; there is no discussion of social or power dimensions. The more recent *ideological model* sees literacy as social and cultural in nature, an integral part of people's daily lives: in some societies, the most important function of literacy is to be able to access religious texts (Rosowsky, 2008); in others reading is undertaken mainly for informational purposes, such as following instructions or reading price tags (Heath, 1983). In this view, often there is a power dimension: some kinds of interaction with print are privileged over others. Many teachers, for instance, are happy to share novels by authors such as Jane Austen or Aldous Huxley but would discourage the reading of comics and graphic novels. These different theoretical framings of literacy are reflected in contrasting methods of literacy teaching, explored in Chapter 5.

The New Literacy Studies movement (New London Group, 1996; Pahl & Rowsell, 2006) builds upon the foundations of the ideological model. Its adherents argue that, in a rapidly changing world, we need to shift from the narrow, traditional focus in the North on one dominant language and culture to a broader vision that embraces cultural and linguistic diversity. For instance, in English-speaking societies, schools tend to attach sole importance to literacy in English and to be ignorant about, or dismissive of, children's experiences of literacy in minority languages. We also need to take account of the multimodal meaning-making opportunities offered by new communications technologies such as SMS, emails, instant messaging and web pages. The time has come then, to talk in terms of *multiliteracies* rather than 'literacy'. The implications of this approach for teachers are discussed in greater detail in Chapter 6.

What are the issues for literacy in more than one language?

We tend to talk about both multilingualism and literacy in polar terms, such as monolingual versus bilingual individuals and oral versus literate societies. Much like speaking a language, however, literacy is not an all or nothing matter. Take the case of Oum Fatima, a

Moroccan woman who had never been to school and therefore could not read and write or do simple arithmetic on paper (Wagner, 1993). She could, however, take letters delivered by the mailman to the appropriate addressee by recognizing the script – Arabic or French – and her mental arithmetic and bargaining skills were legendary. Examples such as Oum Fatima make it clear that we are dealing with a continuum of literacy and not a binary distinction between literate and illiterate.

When dealing with literacy in two or more languages the situation becomes more complex still. Hornberger (2003) talks in terms of 12 intersecting and nested continua of biliteracy organized in four clusters (see Figure 4.1).

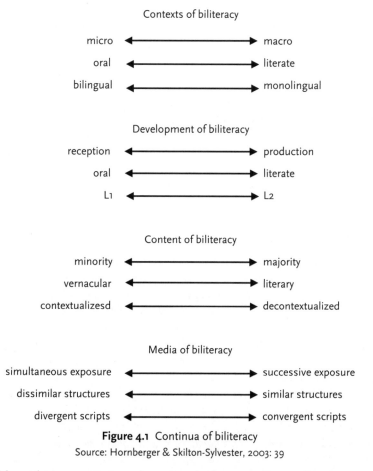

Figure 4.1 Continua of biliteracy
Source: Hornberger & Skilton-Sylvester, 2003: 39

The first of these clusters, *context*, can be approached on a continuum from macro to micro. An example of biliteracy at the micro end would be a Chinese-speaking child in Australia using a bilingual dictionary to learn new vocabulary in English; an example at the macro end would be the Gujarati-speaking Indian community in the UK where people make only minimal use of Gujarati in writing. Context also influences the choices speakers make about the medium of communication – oral or written – and the choice of language for different kinds of writing – L1, L2 or both.

The second group of continua is concerned with the *biliterate development* of individuals. Traditionally, it was assumed that the different language skills (speaking, listening, reading, writing) were acquired in a given order, with the receptive skills of listening and reading preceding the productive skills of speaking and writing. More recently, this relationship has been viewed as bidirectional, with progress in either area leading to progress in the other. For this reason, it is more realistic to think in terms of a receptive–productive continuum. In a similar way, there are continuities between the development of oral and written language. For instance, children may learn to read a second language (in the sense of decoding) before they have gained full control of either the oral or the written systems of the language. A third influence on biliterate development, the L1–L2 transfer continuum, centers on the close connections between development in the different languages spoken by an individual. As pointed out in the discussion of common underlying proficiency in Chapter 2, a child who learns that print is associated with meaning in one language does not have to relearn this concept in the second language.

The *content* of biliteracy can be placed along a continuum of minority and majority languages: a child of Mexican heritage reading in Spanish in the US, for instance, would be dealing with minority language content; in Mexico, Spanish would be the majority language. Similarly, children who engage enthusiastically in the 'vernacular literacy' associated with letter writing or chat rooms may – or may not – display similar levels of engagement with the more literary texts associated with school. Content can also be placed on a continuum from contextualized to decontextualized, the most contextualized pole drawing heavily on the children's own experiences, the most decontextualized bearing little relationship to children's lives outside the classroom.

The final cluster concerns the *media* of biliteracy. Individuals become biliterate in many different ways along a continuum of simultaneous–successive exposure. L2 literacy can follow on varying degrees of literacy in the L1: in the transitional bilingual programmes in the US discussed in Chapter 3, children are taught through the medium of their first language for the first two years before transferring completely to English; in cultural maintenance programs, in contrast, some of the content of the curriculum continues to be taught through the first language. By the same token, L1 literacy can precede varying levels of literacy in the L2, as in French immersion programs in Canada. Languages also lie along a similar–dissimilar continuum in terms of their structure: Jamaican Creole and English, for instance, would be located towards the similar pole; Chinese and English towards the dissimilar pole. Finally, the scripts used to write the languages may be more or less convergent, with pairs such as English and Spanish, which use the same roman script, at the convergent pole and pairs such as Japanese and Spanish located towards the divergent pole.

The various continua do not, of course, operate independently of each other; they should be seen rather as intersecting and nesting.

Case study: Panjabi Sikh literacy practices

Urmi Chana's description of various social and cultural factors which shape the acquisition of literacy in Panjabi in six children aged between eight and 12 makes it clear that we are dealing with a highly complex process that varies not only from one community to the next, but also within the same community. The children concerned were all born in Southall in southern England. They were attending schools where English was the only medium of instruction and were learning to read and write Panjabi, mainly outside school. Their parents who had been born and educated in various locations – the UK, India and Kenya – had varying levels of literacy in English and Panjabi. Although the grandparents were literate in Panjabi, not all lived close by; their accessibility thus affected their ability to offer support for literacy learning.

Family A

This family comprised two paternal grandparents, two parents and two sons, aged 12 and 10. Both grandparents were literate in Panjabi, and the grandfather was also highly literate in Urdu and to some degree in English. The parents were born and educated in Kenya where Panjabi was taught as a subject; they were therefore literate in both languages.

The boys had attended Panjabi class once a week since the age of five. The older boy was studying Panjabi as a subject at secondary school. A tutor came to the house once a week to teach both children the harmonium and singing. The songs were written in the Gurmukhi script used by Sikhs, so Panjabi literacy was central to this activity. The boys regularly took part, as pupils at the Sunday school at the gurdwara [temple], in cultural and religious events of various kinds: festival processions, exhibitions, musical recitals (instrumental and vocal) and sports competitions.

The children's mother taught Panjabi at the Sunday school based in the gurdwara. Their father had recently founded a Sikh scout group in the area, enlisting the help and involvement of friends. Both boys were attending this scout group where they met up with other Panjabi-speaking children. Although English was the dominant language, there were opportunities for talk in both languages.

In summary then, the language environment for the two boys was heavily supportive of both English and Panjabi development.

Family B

The children (aged 11 and 10) in Family B had fewer opportunities to use Panjabi. Close relatives all lived overseas. The older boy still chose to speak Panjabi; his younger brother spoke English except when reciting prayers or reading his Sunday school Panjabi book with his parents. The boys had attended the weekly Panjabi classes regularly since they were seven and eight years old, and played some part in events organized by the Sunday school. This family was less actively involved in gurdwara activities than Family A.

Their network of relatives in England was relatively small. The children's grandparents were in India and contact with other relatives was mostly by phone. The mother had been educated in India and was literate in Panjabi and, to a lesser extent, English. She spoke Panjabi unless the situation required English. Although her lack of confidence in English meant that she was unable to help her children with their homework, she always talked to them about their books in Panjabi. The father had been born in India but received much of his secondary schooling in England. He spoke English and Panjabi to the children. Though he knew some basics of Gurmukhi when he left India, he reported that he had made most progress in reading and writing Panjabi since coming to England through his own efforts.

The children in this family had parents who were as concerned as the parents in Family A to do what they could to support their children. They differed in having far fewer resources at hand – both human and material.

Family C

Children in Family C had a very different language environment. Both parents had been brought up and educated in Britain, were confident speakers of English and Panjabi but were literate only in English. They had the opportunity to speak Panjabi at work but usually spoke English at home. The grandparents lived some distance away and were seen during holidays or at weekends. The family was not involved in gurdwara activities on a regular basis, but attended from time to time.

The two girls, aged 12 and eight, had been going to a Panjabi class run by a private tutor in her own home for 45 minutes every weekday for the last two years. The children were doing work from a series of textbooks, under her direction. The older girl was also learning Panjabi at secondary school where she was expected to take a formal examination two years earlier than usual. Although the mother felt she could not help them as much as if she herself were literate in Panjabi, she believed that they were learning well and wanted to do as much as she could to support them: she found out about the classes, arranged for the girls to attend and bought or borrowed Panjabi books from the local library.

The case study families thus exemplify the diversity of Panjabi language learning experience in the Sikh community. The learning environments range from those with wide and firmly established familial and community networks to those with little support. The reasons parents give for setting their children on the course to biliteracy relate quite clearly, and not surprisingly, to cultural and religious affiliations. But not exclusively so; parents in all three families cited the learning of languages as advantageous in the modern world.

How is biliteracy best developed?

In Chapter 2 we discussed the many advantages of bilingualism for both the individual and the society. Bilinguals who are also biliterate find themselves in an even more favourable position. In settings where education is delivered exclusively or predominantly through the medium of one language, however, biliteracy is much harder to achieve. While speech is an almost constant feature of everyday life, exposure to the written word – and opportunities to develop the relevant competencies – are more variable.

Two factors would appear to determine educational outcomes in multilingual settings: the status of the first language (majority or minority) and the focus of the language-in-education policy (additive or subtractive bilingualism). As we saw in Chapter 3, in programmes where the aim is subtractive bilingualism, minority languages are either excluded from the classroom or used only as a transitional support until students can function in the dominant language. Longitudinal studies show that children educated in this way tend to underperform in relation to their monolingual peers (Baker, 2006). In contrast, minority language speakers who have the opportunity to use both languages over an extended period of time, as for instance, in the case of late-exit bilingual programs, tend to achieve average or above average outcomes (Thomas & Collier, 2002).

For children whose first language is the majority language, the aim is additive bilingualism. This can be achieved in many different ways. Occasionally, multilingualism is sanctioned by the state: in Luxembourg, for instance, where French, German and Letzebuergesch are all official languages, children are expected to be able to function in all three. More often, parents elect to send their children to schools that offer meaningful exposure to other languages, such as the 'European schools' jointly controlled by European Union member states or immersion programmes in Canada and Wales. In all cases, the educational outcomes are positive: children achieve levels of literacy in the dominant language comparable with those of monolingual speakers; their achievement in second and subsequent languages is superior to that of children who have learned the second language as a subject.

So how do we explain these patterns of performance? Many of the theories which relate to biliteracy, of course, apply equally to bilingualism. Jim Cummins has been a pivotal figure in ongoing debates in this area (Baker & Hornberger, 2001; Cummins, 2001). Although his ideas have sometimes provoked fierce debate, his contributions have been invaluable in helping us arrive at a deeper understanding of the issues. Key concepts are discussed below.

The Interdependence Hypothesis

The Interdependence Hypothesis proposes that, given adequate exposure and motivation to learn the majority language, transfer will take place from the majority to the minority language. The mechanisms for this process are explained by the Common Underlying Proficiency model (see Chapter 1): although surface features, such as grammar and vocabulary, vary considerably from one language to another, they are nonetheless integrated in a single thought process. For this reason, information processing, literacy and other cognitive skills can be transferred from one language to another and do not need to be learned afresh for each new language. This is why, for instance, there is no reason to suppose that learning to read simultaneously in two languages should pose problems.

The Threshold Theory

The Threshold Theory examines the relationships between *degrees* of bilingualism and cognition. Two thresholds are proposed, each with cognitive and educational consequences: the first threshold needs to be passed in order to avoid the possible negative consequences of bilingualism, the second threshold in order to experience its positive effects. This theory predicts that the more developed the first language, the easier it will be to develop the second language and vice versa. When children are taught through an underdeveloped second language, their common underlying proficiency will not operate to best effect.

The Developmental Interdependence Hypothesis

The Developmental Interdependence Hypothesis is a further development of the Threshold Theory which looks more closely at the relationship between a bilingual's two languages. It proposes that competence in the child's second language (L2) is partly dependent on the level of competence in the first language (L1) in such a way that the more developed the L1, the easier it will be to develop the L2.

If this hypothesis is correct, it follows that schools which draw only on a bilingual child's second language will not be able to build on their L1 development. The research evidence suggests that this is, indeed, the case. In a study of 2300 Spanish-speaking students over four years for example, Ramírez *et al.* (1991) found late-exit bilingual programmes where students had been taught predominantly in Spanish for four to six years achieved better gains in mathematics, English language skills and English reading than early-exit programs lasting one to two years. Their findings also indicated that minority language students who receive most of their education in English are more likely to fall behind and drop out of school.

Further support for this position comes from an even larger-scale project undertaken by Thomas and Collier (2002) which compared the academic outcomes for different kinds of US bilingual program, including full immersion programs in a minority language, dual-medium or two-way programs, where both a minority and majority language were used as the medium of instruction, transitional bilingual education programs, ESL (English as a second language) programs, and mainstream submersion (English-only) programs. The amount of formal L1 schooling emerged as the strongest predictor of L2 student achievement: the more L1 grade-level schooling, the higher L2 achievement.

It might seem logical to generalize from these findings that the failure to build on children's L1 will be detrimental to educational achievement in all cases. There are, however, important exceptions. Limited use of the L1 is associated with *subtractive* bilingualism where the effect is to replace the use of one language with another. In other contexts, such as French immersion education in Quebec and Welsh-medium education in Wales, the aim is additive, in other words to promote and acknowledge bilingualism and its attendant benefits. The educational outcomes for children in these and a wide range of other additive contexts shows clearly that children in bilingual programs achieve levels in the L2 which are comparable to those of their peers who are taught exclusively in the L2, while their proficiency in the L1 is higher.

Conversational versus academic language proficiency

Cummins has also proposed a distinction between conversational and academic language proficiency. Conversational proficiency develops rapidly over a period of one to two years through face-to-face interaction where there is plenty of contextual support for understanding in the form, for instance, of non-verbal cues. Academic language proficiency, in contrast, is associated with academically demanding subject matter where, typically, there is a great deal less contextual support and acquisition is a much longer process – estimates vary from five to nine years. Children are often offered additional help only until they have developed conversational fluency. Yet, in classroom activities such as synthesis, analysis and evaluation which demand higher-order thinking skills, the absence of contextual support is likely to place students operating in a second or third language at a disadvantage.

Cummins' theory building has important implications for those wishing to promote children's biliterate development (see Figure 4.2).

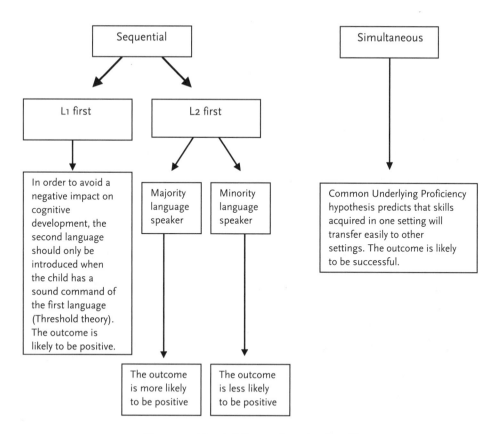

Figure 4.2 How is biliteracy best developed?

Key points

Our understandings of literacy have changed considerably over time. Traditional views of literacy as a set of technical skills (the autonomous model) have given way to the notion of literacy as a social and cultural phenomenon, an integral part of our daily lives (the ideological model). As our thinking on this matter evolves, there has been a further move from 'literacy' to 'multiliteracies', a broader vision that embraces cultural and linguistic diversity as well as the multimodal channels of communication created by the new technologies.

Like multilingualism, biliteracy is a highly complex phenomenon, best described in terms of a series of intersecting and nesting continua.

Various theories of bilingual development have implications for biliteracy and help us to understand the approaches which are likely to have the most successful outcomes. Most notably:

- The **Interdependence Hypothesis** proposes that, given adequate exposure and motivation to learn the majority language, transfer will take place from the majority to the minority language.

- According to the **Common Underlying Proficiency Theory**, although surface features, such as grammar and vocabulary, vary considerably from one language to another, they are integrated in a single thought process. Thus, information processing, literacy and other cognitive skills can be transferred from one language to another and do not need to be learned afresh for each new language.

- The **Threshold Theory** proposes two thresholds: the first needs to be passed to avoid negative consequences of bilingualism; the second to benefit from its positive effects.

- The **Developmental Interdependence Hypothesis** predicts that, when the aim of the school is subtractive bilingualism, the more developed the L1, the easier it will be to develop the L2; schools which draw only on a bilingual child's L2 will thus not be able to build on their L1 development. When the aim of the school is additive bilingualism this would appear not to be the case: contextual factors, such as the status of the majority language come into play.

- **Conversational proficiency** develops rapidly over a period of one to two years through face-to-face interaction where there is plenty of contextual support for understanding in the form, for instance, of non-verbal cues. There is a great deal less contextual support, however, for the development of **Academic language proficiency**, which, typically, is a much longer process.

Activities and discussion points

1. If you are literate in another language, mark the points on Nancy Hornberger's **Continua of literacy** model which correspond to your own experience.

    If you are literate in English only, use the model as a starting point for an interview which encourages someone with biliterate skills to reflect on their experience.

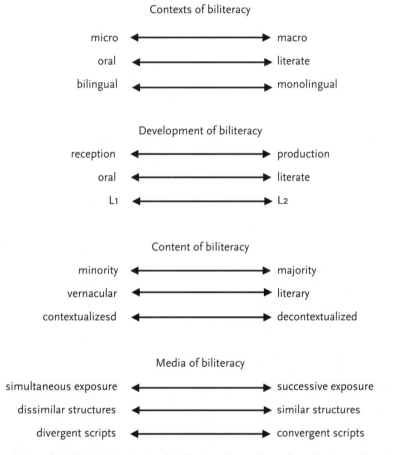

Contexts of biliteracy

micro ←——————————→ macro

oral ←——————————→ literate

bilingual ←——————————→ monolingual

Development of biliteracy

reception ←——————————→ production

oral ←——————————→ literate

L1 ←——————————→ L2

Content of biliteracy

minority ←——————————→ majority

vernacular ←——————————→ literary

contextualizesd ←——————————→ decontextualized

Media of biliteracy

simultaneous exposure ←——————————→ successive exposure

dissimilar structures ←——————————→ similar structures

divergent scripts ←——————————→ convergent scripts

2. Many teachers feel that comics and other forms of popular culture have no place in the classroom. Is this concern legitimate?

Further reading

Literacy

Street, B. & Hornberger, N. (eds) (2007) *Literacy. Encyclopedia of Language and Education*, Vol. 2. Dordrecht: Kluwer.

Literacy online: www.literacyonline.org/Projects/explorer/index.html
This web site is designed to give you an overview of literacy and basic education issues and practices in an international context.

UNESCO literacy portal: http://portal.unesco.org/education/en/ev.php-URL_ID=53553&URL_DO=DO_TOPIC&URL_SECTION=201.html

Multiliteracies

The New London Group (1996) A Pedagogy of Multiliteracies Designing Social Futures. *Harvard Educational Review* 66 (1). Retrieved from: wwwstatic.kern.org/filer/blogWrite44ManilaWebsite/paul/articles/A_Pedagogy_of_Multiliteracies_Designing_Social_Futures.htm

Pahl, K. & Rowsell, J. (2006) *Travel Notes from the New Literacy Studies: Instances of Practice*. Clevedon: Multilingual Matters.

Biliteracy

Hornberger, N. (ed.) (2003) *Continua of Biliteracy: An Ecological Framework for Educational Policy, Research and Practice in Multilingual Settings*. Clevedon: Multilingual Matters.

The writings of Jim Cummins

Baker, C. & Hornberger, N. (2001) *An Introductory Reader to the Writings of Jim Cummins*. Clevedon: Multilingual Matters.

Jim Cummins' ESL and Second Language Learning Web http://iteachilearn.com/cummins/

5

The politics and practice of literacy teaching

This chapter draws on the findings of research on literacy teaching which are relevant to teachers who wish to nurture biliterate development in their classrooms.

- Using the example of the current debate on phonics teaching, it offers evidence that, far from being a neutral activity, decisions about the best approaches to literacy teaching have been appropriated by politicians and suggests why this may be the case.

- It argues that the development of phonological and phonemic awareness, two processes considered important for successful reading, is a more complex issue for children learning to read in an additional language.

- It explains the principles which underlie different writing systems and explores their influence on the development of reading and writing.

- It considers which approaches to teaching are likely to be most productive for children learning to read in a second language.

- Finally, it looks at what we know about learning to write in a second language.

Language, literacy and power

It is a reasonable assumption that decisions about how theory is translated into classroom practice should be the responsibility of teachers. In practice, however, politicians have appropriated this territory.

A few brief historical examples may help to explain why this should be the case. In 17th century Wales, Circulating Schools were established to teach reading to adults and children. The primary aim of the religious bodies responsible for the schools, however, was not to liberate the masses but to enforce obedience to the moral and social code (Jenkins, 1993). Similarly, in the years following the US Civil War, freed slaves had no political voice: before emancipation, it had been illegal to teach slaves to read, and the ability to read and write determined the right to vote (Williams, 2007). The introduction of mass schooling in the 19th century has also been linked with social control: it was argued that literacy learning by the working classes outside school was uncontrolled, and could potentially lead to increased radicalization. Mass schooling, in contrast, could be employed to control the ways in which literacy was used (Graff, 1991).

Similar critiques have been applied to current literacy teaching initiatives. Many policy-makers, funders and employers in the developed world consider literacy to be central to helping people to find and retain employment. Writers such as Auerbach (1992) and Gee (1991), in contrast, argue that race and gender play a greater role in shaping economic prospects than literacy; it is often the very 'different-ness' of minorities that limits access to education and other resources associated with economic progress. Life chances are further constrained when individuals consistently denied privilege and power internalize this oppression, believing that they are 'unworthy'.

The causal link between literacy and economic development is also contested in developing countries. Writers such as Wagner (1999) question whether literacy is a cause or consequence of economic growth, or even whether the two are related at all. The reliability of data used in analyses of literacy rates and economic growth is also problematic, raising doubts about the usefulness of comparisons.

The quest for the Holy Grail of literacy – the most effective way of teaching children to read – dates back to the 16th century (Davies, 1973). The contemporary debate, however, centers on the relative importance of 'part-to-whole' and 'whole-to-part' approaches. Let's look first at the technical and philosophical differences between the two approaches and then at the way in which politicians have appropriated the debate.

'Phonics' versus 'Whole Language'

Advocates of 'part-to-whole' approaches stress the importance of the explicit teaching of a set of skills (the parts). The two main examples of this approach are phonics, which involves an understanding of the relationship between sounds and symbols, and 'Look and say', or the rapid recognition of whole words in isolation. When learning to read, the skills required include the ability to recognize letters, spelling patterns and whole words; when put together, these skills allow children to *decode* a text. When learning to write, children follow a similar process: they start with letters (or graphemes) which they build into words, then sentences and longer texts. Thus, for teachers using a phonics approach, the task in reading is to break down a word such as *big* into its letters, pronounce a phoneme for each letter in turn /b, i, g/, and blend the phonemes to form a word. In teaching children to write, the sequence is reversed. Children say the word they want to write, segment it into its phonemes, say each in turn, then write a grapheme for each phoneme to produce the written word. The direct explicit teaching associated with part-to-whole approaches is grounded in behaviorist theory and emphasizes *what* is to be taught and *how*.

In contrast, proponents of whole-to-part (or 'whole language') approaches believe that sound-letter correspondences are best taught in context. The focus, then, is not on the mechanical decoding of the written word but on equipping children with the strategies they need to make meaning of a text. In this view, understanding depends not only on our ability to decode but also on our knowledge of how language works and of the world. Children need to use a wide range of cuing systems – grapho-phonic, lexical, syntactic and semantic – to make meaning of text in what has been termed a 'psycholinguistic guessing game' (Goodman, 1967).

Similarly, advocates of whole language believe that children learn to write by reinventing the writing system for themselves: observing, generating hypotheses about how to do things, trying these out, and evaluating their efforts against examples of conventional writing. In the process, they come to understand the difference between drawing and writing, and that letters represent words; they also invent spellings and punctuation. Whole language approaches are influenced by constructivism, a theory of knowing and learning which views the learner as an active contributor and seeks teaching methods which focus on the student.

There are, of course, areas of overlap. While advocates of the two approaches differ in their views as to how children learn to read, both recognize the importance of the relationships between letters and sounds, and share the belief that understanding is the ultimate goal of reading instruction.

Many writers point to the unnecessary polarization in the debate about teaching methods and, by the late 1980s, there was strong support across the English-speaking world for the notion that no one method of teaching reading was suitable for all children: a balanced approach, using a variety of methods, was required. While most educationalists have continued to promote the benefits of a balanced approach, the pendulum has swung increasingly towards the teaching of phonics.

The political debate

The phonics debate needs to be placed in a broader political context. At a time when explicit links are being made between the 'products' of schooling, the labor market and national economic performance (Soler, 2001), politicians and legislators have appropriated debates on the philosophy and methodology of literacy teaching which, traditionally, were the territory of academics. Paterson (2000) reports how 101 US bills encouraging or mandating phonics instruction had been introduced in state legislatures since 1990. These initiatives tend to be associated with Republican legislators; the Christian Right has even promoted a number of specifically Christian phonics programs as the only spiritually and educationally sound reading instruction method (see, for instance, www.veritaspress.com). Opposition to these developments, however, has been gathering momentum and has centered on the exaggerated importance attached to phonics instruction by the highly influential US National Reading Panel (NRP) (2000) (Allington, 2002; Coles, 2003; Pearson, 2004).

Literacy has attracted similar attention from the New Labour administration in the UK where successive revisions to flagship education policies have placed increasing emphasis on phonics. Discussion has centered not only on the relative importance of phonics but on *which* phonics approach is most effective, with the findings of two recent longitudinal studies (Grant, 2005; Johnston & Watson, 2005) providing support for *synthetic* rather than *analytic* phonics. In synthetic phonics, children learn to recognize the graphemes which correspond to the phonemes of English (up to 44 in number depending on accent); they then sound out each phoneme in the word, e.g. *kuh-ah-tuh: cat*. In analytic phonics, words are split into smaller parts to help with decoding: the onset (or initial sound) and the rime (which makes up the remainder of the word or syllable), as in *b-ig: big*.

Against a growing clamour from the Reading Reform Foundation, a lobby group which advocates 'synthetic phonics first, fast and only' (Chew, 2005), the Shadow Education Secretary announced in April 2005 that, under a Conservative government, all children in England would learn to read using a synthetic phonics approach. In March 2006, the Education Secretary endorsed the teaching of synthetic phonics following the publication of the *Independent review of the teaching of reading* (Rose, 2006). Perplexingly, this report ignored the findings of a systematic review of research on approaches to the teaching of phonics (Torgerson *et al.*, 2006), published three months earlier and commissioned by the same government department, which found no evidence either for or against the use of synthetic phonics. Whatever the rationale for this decision, the political implications are clear: this course of action – by accident or design – neutralized a potential vote winning advantage for the Conservative party.

Research evidence on phonics teaching

There is a growing consensus that evidence-based research should underpin educational policy. In commissioning reviews of the research, the UK government followed in the wake of the National Reading Panel in the US (NRP, 2000); the Aoateroa/New Zealand House of Representatives' Inquiry into the Teaching of Reading (Education and Science Committee, 2001); and the National Inquiry into the Teaching of Literacy in Australia (Australia, 2005).

Reviews of research fall in two main categories: systematic and narrative. Systematic reviews use explicit methods and prespecified criteria to identify studies for meta-analysis (a method of statistically summarizing quantitative outcomes from a range of studies). Their aim is to increase the validity of the findings through transparency in both the selection of studies and methods of analysis. Such studies are not, however, without problems:

- *Issues of interpretation* There were important differences in emphasis when Camilli *et al.* (2003) reanalyzed essentially the same studies as those included in the National Reading Panel meta-analysis.

- *Insufficient data* When Torgerson *et al.* (2006) attempted to further refine the criteria for selection of studies, they were unable to answer several of their research questions because so few studies met the strict criteria.

- *Unduly narrow focus* Meta-analyses, by definition, focus on quantitative research which many writers believe oversimplifies the highly complex world of the classroom.

- *Danger of overgeneralization* Many experimental studies involve relatively few hours of instruction and are delivered by a researcher or person other than the classroom teacher (Solity, 2003). It is unwise to generalize from these studies to what happens with real-life classrooms.

Most literature reviews take a more narrative approach, reporting on studies undertaken from a range of theoretical positions, both qualitative and quantitative (see, for instance, Australian Government, 2005; Ellis, 2005; Purdie & Ellis, 2005). Narrative reviews also have inherent weaknesses, including bias in both the selection of studies and their interpretation.

Despite considerable polarization, the consensus emerging from the various reviews of research is that systematic phonics instruction is a *necessary* but not *sufficient* condition for the teaching of reading. There is no convincing evidence either for or against synthetic as opposed to analytic phonics (Ellis, 2005; Torgerson *et al.*, 2006). The weight of opinion thus favors a balanced approach, incorporating both constructivist strategies and direct instruction, over either whole-language or phonics approaches used in isolation. The crisis over pedagogy appears to be more manufactured that real.

How do bilingual students learn to read?

We need to broaden the discussion now from phonics to other matters of relevance for bilingual learners. In English-speaking countries, literacy learning is approached very much from a monolingual perspective; at the policy level, at least, awareness of the challenges for second language learners is limited. In the National Inquiry into the Teaching of Reading in Australia (Australia, 2005), for instance, 'English as a second language' appears only in a glossary and as bullet points in two places in the appendices. This absence of discussion perhaps reflects the unsatisfactory nature of much of the research. Many studies fail to distinguish between different groups of bilingual learners or to take into consideration issues such as: which languages do children use? Which language is dominant? What is the relationship between the spoken and written languages? Where have children learned to read the languages – at home or in school? (Edwards & Rassool, 2007). If the research design fails to address issues of this kind, the validity and generalizability of the findings are clearly open to question.

So what does the research tell us about bilingual learners? Several areas have attracted considerable attention, including phonological and phonemic awareness; the principles underlying writing systems; the influence of writing systems on reading; and the strategies of bilingual readers.

Phonological and phonemic awareness

Cognitive and developmental psychologists have shown considerable interest in phonological awareness – the ability to distinguish speech features such as syllables and rhyme – because of its strong relationship with success in learning to read. Typically, tests administered to children focus on issues such as 'How many syllables are there in *caterpillar?*' or 'Which of the following words rhyme with 'shoe': toe, too, she?' Three main themes in the research literature are of relevance for bilingual children. First, exposure to more than one language appears to increase phonological awareness. Second, the structure of the language affects phonological awareness (e.g. children who speak languages with complex initial consonant clusters are better able to isolate initial sounds). Third, phonological awareness in the child's first language is strongly related to reading achievement in the second language and vice versa. The pedagogical implications of this research, however, are unclear: some writers believe there is a causal link between phonological awareness and reading; others maintain that phonological awareness is one of many interesting, but not necessarily causally connected, cognitive correlates of reading and spelling achievement.

Phonemic awareness, a subset of phonological awareness, concerns listeners' ability to perceive and manipulate phonemes, the smallest meaningful elements of sound in words. While it is widely believed that it is beneficial to focus on phonemic awareness in reading programmes in the first year of formal schooling, the usefulness of this course of action in multilingual settings is open to question. Take the following examples:

Two phonemes in English, one in Spanish
In English, [d], as in *Dan*, and [ð] as in *than* are two separate phonemes. In Spanish, they are one: in words such as /dado/(given), the initial /d/ is always pronounced as [d] at the beginning of a word and as [ð] in the middle or at the end.

One phoneme is English, two phonemes in Panjabi
In English, /k/ is aspirated (or followed by a puff of air) at the beginning of a word, but not in the middle or the end. In Panjabi, both variants can occur at any point in the word, [pʰul], for instance, means 'fruit' while [pul] means 'moment'.

Unstressed vowels in English
Most English phonological awareness activities use monosyllabic words. They therefore neatly sidestep the question of multisyllabic words where unstressed vowels are reduced to schwa [ə]. Although spelled the same, the first vowel in photograph, for instance, is different from the first vowel in photographer.

The inevitable conclusion is that children in the process of learning English will experience greater difficulty in reading unfamiliar words than native speakers who already know how words are pronounced.

Writing systems

The challenges of learning to read and write vary to some extent according to which writing system is used. Although languages are encoded in a very wide variety of ways, writing systems are underpinned by a much smaller number of organizing principles. As illustrated in Figure 5.1, the main division is between sound-based and meaning-based systems. In turn, sound-based systems can be based on syllables or phonemes and phonemic systems can be further subdivided into consonantal and alphabetic scripts.

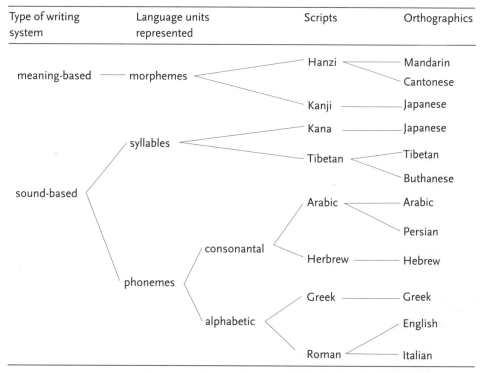

Figure 5.1 Major types of writing system (adapted from Cook & Bassetti, 2005: 5)

Alphabets

An alphabet – a term derived from the first two letters of the Greek alphabet – is a set of letters which – singly or in combination – represents the phonemes of a spoken language either as they are today or as they were in the past. The best-known alphabets – the Latin (or Roman) and the Cyrillic – have been adapted to write many different languages. Most other alphabets, e.g. Greek, are used for just one or a small number of languages.

Consonantal systems (abjads)

Consonantal systems or abjads usually contain only consonants. Occasionally vowels are indicated in special kinds of texts, such as religious writings or books for children, usually with diacritics above or below the line.

One of the best-known abjads is Arabic. It runs from right to left and has several variants of each letter, depending on their position in the word – initial, medial, final or isolated (see Figure 5.2). To cope with such a large number of variant forms, some word processing programs offer 'contextual analysis'. This means that the correct character variant for any given position in the word appears automatically. Other abjads include Hebrew.

ـ	ـ	ـ	ـ	b
ـ	ـ	ـ	ـ	p
ـ	ـ	ـ	ـ	t
ـ	ـ	ـ	ـ	t
ـ	ـ	ـ	ـ	s
ج	ج	ج	ج	j
ج	ج	ج	ج	ch
ح	ح	ح	ح	h
خ	خ	خ	خ	x

Figure 5.2 Independent, initial, medial and final forms of selected Arabic letters

Syllabic writing systems

The organizing principle of syllabic writing systems (or abugidas) is the syllable. Those starting with the same consonant are based on the same symbol, which is then modified according to the vowel. The combination of vowel and consonant forms a single symbol. For instance, instead of a single symbol for 'p', you find separate letters for 'pā', 'pa' 'pi', 'pi', etc (see Figure 5.3).

Figure 5.3 Letters for *pa, pā, pi, pi* in the Devanagari script

Most of the Indic scripts, including Bengali, Gujarati, Hindi and Panjabi, are abugidas. So, too, is the Thai writing system.

Meaning-based systems

Meaning-based writing systems make direct links between written symbols and meaning. The best-known example is Chinese, which represents meaning using four main kinds of character.

- *Pictograms* resembling the things they represent which have become increasingly stylized over the years (Figure 5.4). Only a small proportion of characters are pictograms but they tend to represent words that are used frequently.

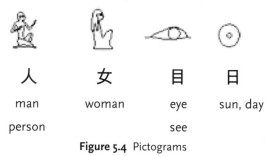

人	女	目	日
man	woman	eye	sun, day
person		see	

Figure 5.4 Pictograms

- *Ideograms* (Figure 5.5), also few in number and frequently used, graphically represent abstract ideas:

—	二	三	中
one	two	three	middle

Figure 5.5 Ideograms

- *Semantic–phonetic compound characters* (Figure 5.6) consist of a semantic element (or radical), which suggests their meaning, and a phonetic element, which suggests their pronunciation. This kind of character makes up an estimated 90% of all characters. Below are some of the compound characters which share a semantic element (on the left) meaning 'water'.

浴 yu (bath)

江 jiang (river)

洋 yang (ocean)

海 hai (sea)

油 you (oil)

Figure 5.6 Semantic–phonetic compound characters

- *Semantic–semantic compounds* made up of two independent characters on the basis of meaning (e.g. peace = roof and woman).

In the initial stages of learning to read, however, children in the People's Republic of China use pinyin, one of several systems that draws on letters from the roman alphabet to represent the sounds of Mandarin, as a kind of aide-memoire (see Figure 5.7).

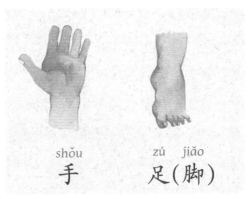

Figure 5.7 A page from an early reader with pinyin transcription

The influence of writing systems on reading

As we have seen, all writing systems – and even Chinese – reflect to some extent the phonology or the sound system of the language they are representing. Equally, all writing systems reflect information about the linguistic structure of the language. In English, for instance, the plural marker in dogs, cats and horses is represented with -s, despite the fact that this is pronounced differently in each case [cats, dogz, horsiz]. The differences thus lie in the extent to which writing systems reflect either phonology or morphology (the structure and form of words). Deep writing systems focus on morphemes; shallow writing systems are based on phonemes. There is variation, however, even within the same writing system. Italian orthography, for instance, is much shallower than English: the sound-letter correspondences are much more regular.

The evidence suggests that, for European languages, depth and syllable complexity affect the rate at which children learn to read (Seymour, 2005). At one pole, English and Dutch both have deep orthographies (or language-specific rules of spelling) and complex syllable structures and take longest; at the other pole, Italian has a shallow orthography and a simple syllable structure. Between these poles lie languages like Portuguese and French with shallow orthographies and complex syllable structures.

Speed of reading acquisition is one issue; specific difficulties in learning to read is another. Because dyslexia is associated with phonological rather than visual deficits in alphabetic languages (Caravolas, 2005), it is sometimes assumed that this disorder does not occur in meaning-based systems such as Chinese. This would appear not to be the case for two reasons. First, all writing systems map orthography to phonology to some extent: as indicated earlier, many Chinese characters include information on sound. Second, dyslexia is a complex phenomenon with visual as well as auditory components.

What, then, are the implications of differences between writing systems and orthographies for teaching methodologies? Taking the example of English, Trudell and Schroeder (2007) identify several techniques well suited to the deep orthography of English, including word recognition, the teaching of complex but frequent spelling patterns (e.g. -ight) and the use of context cues. By the same token, they argue that the shallower orthography used in Bantu languages, together with linguistic features such as the use of tone and multisyllabic words, require specific teaching strategies, including early focus on phonological awareness, and practice with syllable recognition and connecting long series of syllables within words. These language-specific measures are recommended alongside universal approaches such as the development of comprehension skills.

Reading strategies

Second language readers make far greater use than native speakers of grapho-phonic strategies – the reliance on initial letters and sounding out for word identification (Rosowsky, 2001). There are various possible explanations. By the time they start school, native speakers have already developed a wide range of tacit knowledge of how their language works. They will also have heard and used many of the words they encounter in print. The less extensive exposure of learners to the target language means that they may be familiar with some senses of words but not others. Limited knowledge of clause and sentence level grammar may impede reading comprehension, even when individual words have been recognized. The challenge for language learners is thus to develop 'semantic agility' through active inquiry (McWilliam, 1998). Limited exposure to certain text types or genres may also place language learners at a disadvantage, especially if information is structured and presented differently in their other languages.

These observations have important implications for the usefulness of skills-based approaches for children learning to read in a second language. Various writers including Hutchinson *et al.* (2003), Stuart (2004) and Denton *et al.* (2004) caution that undue emphasis should not be placed on decoding at the expense of developing comprehension skills. A growing body of research which focuses on classroom processes rather than outcomes further reinforces the conclusion that undue emphasis on skills-based approaches is unhelpful in multilingual classrooms. González *et al.* (2005), for instance, show how, when teachers placed less emphasis on decoding and more on meaning by offering support for understanding in both English and Spanish, children who had been performing at low levels were able to cope with more difficult texts.

Learning to write in multilingual settings

Reading has received far more attention from researchers in both monolingual and multilingual settings. There is, however, a growing interest in writing.

Children become aware of other writing systems at an early stage. In print-rich societies, children are exposed to a wide variety of environmental print, including street and shop signs, posters, labels, leaflets and cards. Children as young as five or six understand that different writing systems work in different ways. Chinese children, for instance, know that Chinese is not alphabetic and uses characters to represent words; Arabic-speaking children know that

Arabic writing runs from right to left and that the form of letters changes according to their position in the word; and Spanish-speaking children are aware that the same letter sometimes corresponds to different sounds in English and in Spanish (Kenner, 2004).

The 'secretarial' skills – handwriting and spelling – vary considerably from one language to another, as do the approaches to teaching these skills. As the case study which follows demonstrates, Chinese children are taught using methods very different from those usually found in English-speaking classrooms.

Case study: Learning to write in Chinese

Each character has to fit within a notional square and is made up of strokes written in the same direction and in a set order – left to right, top to bottom. Children first practice the 12 basic different strokes, then learn the sequence required to form a particular character. In order to memorize the character, they need a great deal of practice. Lei Ming demonstrates a far greater level of pen control than would be expected in a child of the same age learning to write English (see Figure 5.8); she also shows great visual acuity in being able to recognize small differences in stroke patterns.

Figure 5.8 Lei Ming practices characters

Visualization plays an important part in the teaching of writing. An Ran (2000) reports how one of the mothers in her study draws her daughter's attention to the hook on the left side as she demonstrates 钓, the character for diao (to fish), and reminds her that you can use a hook to catch fish. Another mother draws attention to the shape 弯, the character for wan wan (crescent):

'Wan wan' has got two pointed sides. [Indicates the points on the crescent shape she has drawn]. It looks like a little boat.

She explains 坐, the character for zuo [sit], in a similar way:

One side is a person [人 ren]; the other side is a person [人 ren]. And then you write the 'tu' [soil]. That means that two persons sit on the ground. This is the word 'zuo' [sit]

Learning to write, however, involves not only secretarial skills but composition. This appears to be similar for first and second language learners, providing support for Cummins' theory of interdependence. Hudelson (1989) summarizes the main conclusions emerging from research on English as a second language (ESL) as follows:

1. ESL learners, while they are still learning English, can write; they can create their own meaning.

2. ESL learners can respond to the works of others and can use another learner's responses to their work to make substantive revisions in their creations.

3. Texts produced by ESL writers look very much like those produced by young native speakers. These texts demonstrate that the writers are making predictions about how the written language works. As the writers' predictions change, the texts change.

4. Children approach writing and develop as writers differently from one another.

5. The classroom environment has a significant impact on ESL children's development as writers.

6. Culture may affect the writers' view of writing, of the functions or purposes for writing, and of themselves as writers.

7. The ability to write in the native language facilitates the child's ESL writing in several different ways. Native language writing provides learners with information about the purposes of writing. Writing ability in the native language provides second language learners with both linguistic and non-linguistic resources that they can use as they approach second language writing. In addition, second language learners apply the knowledge about writing gained in first language settings to second language settings.

Further support for a social-constructivist approach to writing comes from evidence of the negative effects of part-to-whole approaches. Hornberger and Skilton-Sylvester (2003) describe how Chamran, a Cambodian child, struggled to decode and to spell during her first three years of schooling in Philadelphia. Most of her assignments involved copying from the board or from a homework sheet. When asked by the researcher if she wanted to write a story, she typically said 'no'. When she finally agreed, she wrote 'Spelling Test' at the top of the page and numbers down the left-hand side from 1 to 15. While she was familiar with the conventions of spelling tests, she was clearly not comfortable with other writing genres. This response was particularly poignant because Chamran did not understand the meaning of the words she was being asked to spell.

In contrast, the experience of the the isiXhosa and Afrikaan-speaking children at Battswood Primary School in Cape Town, described in the case study which follows, was a great deal more positive.

Case study: Battswood Biliteracy Project

For many African language-speaking children, the first introduction to written language is at school. Carole Bloch (2005) describes how most children in South African schools are only able to copy words and sentences by the end of Grade 3. Traditionally, their failure to be 'ready' was largely attributed to a lack of parental and family support and input. No significance was attached to factors such as inadequate teaching approaches, the lack of authentic and appropriate mother tongue reading materials or the absence of a culture of reading and writing.

In the Battswood Biliteracy Project, a mixed class of isiXhosa and English-Afrikaans bilingual children was followed from Grades 1 to 6. IsiXhosa was used as a language of instruction for initial reading and writing, alongside English, which was the official teaching medium of the school. In retrospect, the researchers realized that they should also have used Afrikaans.

Carole Bloch and Ntombizanele Mahobe, an isiXhosa-speaking colleague, wanted to create a print-rich environment in order to motivate the Battswood children, most of whom came from 'low literacy' homes, to read and write for personally meaningful reasons. They did this by hunting for isiXhosa and English stories to create a classroom library and making their own reading materials. They made time each day for the teachers to read stories to the children in both isiXhosa and English and for the children to explore books alone and with friends. They introduced interactive writing as a way to stimulate writing in both languages, risk taking, invented spellings and one-to-one nurturing.

Ntombizanele worked hard at consistently answering or initiating in isiXhosa and at responding thoughtfully in writing to each child. The children, for their part grew to trust her; many shared their concerns and asked for advice. The teacher researchers also worked hard at involving parents and caregivers in reading with the children. They knew that they were expecting a lot: most isiXhosa-speaking families lived very far from the school and would have to struggle to find the taxi or train fare. They came to realize, however, that starting small *is* significant – and that even if just one adult decides to participate, this relationship should be nurtured.

By the time the children reached the end of Grade 6, it had been possible to document the ways in which the children were becoming confident and enthusiastic readers and writers of both isiXhosa and English. Most were able to read and write equally in two languages (though some preferred using one or the other language). Their work showed that the development of children's English competence was not harmed despite the fact that, unlike most African language-speaking children in 'ex-white or coloured' schools, they had experienced a significant proportion of their teaching through isiXhosa.

By working in these ways it was possible to challenge a number of myths: time spent on mother tongue teaching does *not* means less English learning; initial literacy learning does *not* require structured phonics-based methods; and children do *not* become confused if they learn to read and write simultaneously in their mother tongue and English.

Key points

There are two main approaches to literacy teaching:

- The parts-to-whole approach exemplified by phonics which stresses the importance of the explicit teaching of a set of skills. It is grounded in behaviorist theory and focuses on *what* is to be taught and *how*.

- The whole-to-parts (or 'Whole Language') approach considers that sound letter correspondences are best taught in context and the focus is on equipping children with the strategies they need to make meaning of a text. Whole language approaches are influenced by constructivism, a theory which views the learner as an active contributor.

Literacy is not a neutral issue. The case of phonics versus Whole Language teaching illustrates the ways in which politicians have appropriated the debate from educationalists. The consensus emerging from the research is that systematic phonics instruction is a *necessary* but not *sufficient* condition for the teaching of reading. The crisis over pedagogy thus appears to be more manufactured that real.

The fact that many researchers fail to distinguish between different groups of bilingual learners makes it difficult to extrapolate from their findings. However, it is possible to make some broad generalizations:

- The ability of bilingual children to distinguish speech features such as syllables and rhyme (phonological awareness) differs in important respects from that of monolinguals. However, the pedagogical implications of this research are not clear, since there is disagreement as to whether there is a causative relationship between phonological awareness and success in reading and spelling.

- The ability to perceive and manipulate phonemes, the smallest meaningful elements of sound in words (phonemic awareness) is a complex issue for bilinguals. When learning to read in two languages, children may, for instance, encounter situations where two phonemes in their first language correspond to one in the second and vice versa.

- The challenges of learning to read and write can vary according to which writing system is used – alphabetic, consonantal, syllabic or meaning based. While some techniques, such as the development of comprehensions skills, can be applied universally, others need to be sensitive to specific languages and writing systems.

- There are differences even within the same writing system: sound letter correspondences are closer in Italian, for instance, than in English. There is some evidence that children learn to read more rapidly with 'shallow orthographies' like Italian. However, there is no evidence to support the widespread assumption that specific learning difficulties like dyslexia do not occur with meaning-based writing systems like Chinese.

- Because children are less familiar with the vocabulary and structures of the second language, they rely far more on initial letters and sounding out for word identification. It is therefore important to compensate for this tendency to rely too heavily on decoding by helping children to develop strategies which allow allow them to make meaning of the text.

- Children become aware of other writing systems at an early stage and the process of learning to write appears to be similar for first and second language learners.

Activities and discussion points

1. Learning to write a different script requires concentration, hand eye coordination, and an understanding of how characters are formed. Try copying the extracts below.

    Urdu

    پھر عمران کو ایک مشکل پیش آئی۔ وہ بولا میری مدد کرو !

    Gujarati

    પરંતુ હિપોપૉટેમસ્ની એક વાત ચિત્તાને હેરાન કરતી.

    Panjabi

    ਮੇਰੇ ਮਾਤਾ ਜੀ ਨਾਸ਼ਤਾ ਲਿਆ ਰਹੇ ਹਨ ।

    Chinese

    出門時 ， 蓋爾穿上短上衣 。

    Did you find some scripts easier than others? Why?

    How did you feel when you finished writing?

    Did you remember to copy the Urdu script from right to left?

2. Look at the Dutch passage below. Use the illustrations and your knowledge of cognates in English and other languages to help you arrive at what it means. Discuss your ideas with a partner before looking at a translation and commentary on p. 126.

Ik lees graag

Ik heet Irene en ik lees graag.
Ik lees graag longe boeken

Ik lees graag korte boeken

Ik lees graag grappige boeken

Ik lees graag verdrietige boeken

Ik lees graag boeken met plaatjes

Ik lees gewoon graag

Further reading

Literacy and power

Blackledge, A. (2000) *Literacy, Power and Social Justice*. Stoke-on-Trent: Trentham Books.

McCarty, T. (ed.) (2005) *Language, Literacy, and Power in Schooling*. Mahwah, NJ: Lawrence Erlbaum.

The reading process in different languages

Snowling, M. (ed.) (2005) *The Science of Reading: A Handbook*. [Part IV]. Malden, MA: Blackwell.

Learning to read in an additional language

Gregory, E. (2008) *Learning to Read in a New Language: Making Sense of Words and Worlds*. London: Sage.

Phonics

Adams, M.J. (1991) *Beginning to Read: Thinking and Learning About Print*. Cambridge, MA: MIT Press.

Whole language

Goodman, K.S. (2005) *What's Whole in Whole Language: 20th Anniversary Edition*. Muskegon, MI: RDR Books.

Writing systems

Coulmas, F. (2002) *Writing Systems: An Introduction to Their Linguistic Analysis*. Cambridge: Cambridge University Press.

Rogers, H. (2004) *Writing Systems: A Linguistic Approach*. New Malden, MA: Wiley-Blackwell.

Cook, V. & Bassetti, B. (eds) (2005) *Second Language Writing Systems*. Clevedon: Multilingual Matters.

Omniglot: www.omniglot.com
Details of most alphabets and other writing systems currently in use.

Yellow Bridge: www.yellowbridge.com
Provides animated stroke order information for Chinese characters.

Zhongwen: www.zhongwen.com
Chinese characters and culture.

6

Language, literacy and culture

In this chapter we look at the implications of recent research on literacy for our understanding of what happens in multilingual classrooms. We try to answer the following questions:

- What counts as literacy? We challenge the widespread assumption that school-based literacy is the only legitimate way to engage with the written word.

- How do we explain differences in literacy achievement? We show how limited access to officially sanctioned cultural knowledge clearly disadvantages some groups of children.

- How have minorities reacted to their marginalization in schools? We look at community provision aimed at maintaining home languages and cultures in response to dissatisfaction with mainstream schooling.

- How do children reconcile home and school approaches? We examine the learning opportunities offered by contrasting literacy practices.

- How can schools best support children's bilingualism and biliteracy? We explore the ways in which students can be empowered to question dominant beliefs and practices.

What counts as literacy?

Since the 1980s there has been a marked shift in the conceptualization of literacy from a neutral to a political activity. As we have seen in earlier chapters, writers from many different disciplines, disenchanted with the autonomous model of reading (Street, 1997) which was prevalent at the time, began exploring reading and writing in a much wider range of settings than had previously been the case – from everyday life to prisons, and from youth groups to adult literacy. Growing attention is also being paid to multilingual contexts both in and out of school under the umbrella of what is sometimes known as 'New Literacy Studies' (New London Group, 1996; Pahl & Rowsell, 2005). In this approach, skills are learned when used for something personally meaningful or economically useful. The focus, then, is on what people *do with* literacy, rather than on what literacy can *do for* people.

What counts as literacy varies considerably from one cultural setting to another. Heath's (1983) groundbreaking study of the African-American community of Trackton describes patterns of interaction with print very different from those of both the neighboring white working-class neighborhood of Roadville and the middle-class expectations of the school. Trackton children have no books. Encounters with print tend to be functional or problem solving – picking out the relevant parts of instruction booklets so that you can assemble or modify a piece of equipment, or reading the price tags in the local store so that you know you are making a good buy. Anyone who chooses to read alone is dismissed as lacking social skills: reading is considered a social activity. The evening newspaper is usually read aloud on the porch, starting with the obituaries and followed by the job vacancies, advertisements for sale and captions beneath pictures and headlines. Circulars and other letters of general interest are also read aloud and generate a great deal of discussion.

While children from Trackton have no tradition of bedtime stories or sharing books with their parents, they are privy to a rich source of personal narratives and communal wisdom enshrined in proverbs, riddles and story. The rules for African-American storytelling, however, are often very different from what we find in books: they often have no clear beginning or end and go on for as long as the audience is prepared to listen. Smitherman (1997: 147–8) describes this phenomenon as a meandering away from the point which 'takes the listener on episodic journeys and over tributary rhetorical routes, but like the flow of nature's rivers and streams, it all eventually leads back to the source'.

Street's (1984) study of maktab or Qu'rānic literacy in an Iranian village also shows how the skills required are very different from those required in mainstream Western schools. In order to find specific texts to justify an argument, students learn to find their way around religious works by using, for example, headings and contents pages; they recognize passages they have memorized by their position on the page rather than by cracking the phonemic code. Liturgical literacy of this kind is not, of course, restricted to Islam. Non-Hebrew-speaking Jewish children learn to read the Torah as part of the barmitzvah rite of passage; the liturgy of the Coptic Church in Egypt uses a language which has not been spoken for more than 1500 years; and Latin played an important role in the Catholic Church until relatively recently. Rosowsky (2001: 61) argues that such practices are 'saturated with meaning' and that they link participants 'synchronically with the religious community, locally and globally' and 'diachronically with the established history of the religion itself'.

Assumptions of mainstream educators

The new agenda of researchers is not, however, reflected in what is happening in schools: here the focus remains firmly on *literacy* rather than *literacies*; there is little evidence of the influence of New Literacy Studies on education policy. A widespread assumption, embedded in both the 2000 US 'No child left behind' legislation and the 1988 UK Education Act, is that 'equality of opportunity' should be interpreted as the *same* provision for all. One of the consequences of this assumption is that the prior knowledge and learning of many children is marginalized. Critics of the restrictions placed on the use of Spanish in California classrooms, for instance, point out that teachers are unable to build on children's most important learning resources – their language and their cultural experiences – and, in the process, the language and its users assume pariah status (Crawford, 2008; Wright, 2005).

Although our understanding of literacy has expanded considerably in recent years, many educators have little knowledge of what takes place in minority communities. Views are often based on assumptions rather than experience and are presented in a negative light. Roskowsky (2008) argues that Islamic literacy is perceived by teachers mainly for its nuisance value: children use 'I've got to go to the mosque' as an excuse for leaving early when they are placed in detention after schools; and attendance at Qu'rānic classes is seen as intruding on valuable homework time.

Teachers, then, act as gatekeepers, upholding specific norms about language and what counts as knowledge and defining literacy in terms of the practices and expectations of the dominant group. An obvious example is the way that reading difficulties are explained in terms of parental failure to share books with their children from early infancy (DfEE, 1998). Home–school reading initiatives (Topping, 1992) and campaigns such as Bookstart, which aim to raise the achievements of working-class and ethnic minority children, have paid particular attention to instructing parents in this aspect of reading. Increasingly, however, such assumptions are being challenged. Observers such as Kelly *et al.* (2001) question whether book and story-reading experiences at home are, in themselves, essential for success or whether they are important simply because they reproduce what counts in early literacy tuition in school.

The implicit assumption of such campaigns is that those who subscribe to the school model of literacy are the only ones who value literacy. Yet a closer scrutiny of attitudes provides no support for this position, either now or in the past. Islam, for instance, views literacy as an individual religious obligation, not something reserved for the privileged few; and, as well as meeting spiritual requirements, the ability to read the Qu'rān in Arabic is associated with status and respect.

There is certainly no shortage of evidence for the importance attached to literacy by Muslim parents in the West today. While sharing storybooks may not be an important part of parents' interaction with young children, storytelling is widespread. In a study of the home literacy practices of Bangladeshi families in the UK, Blackledge (1999: 189) describes how mothers use a variety of traditional and Islamic sources, as well as ones of their own creation: 'I make up stories for my three boys, like "There were once three princes who became kings", and so on'. They also support their children's more formal literacy learning: 'As often as I can I will spend twenty minutes teaching them Bengali'; 'I sit with the children for two hours on Saturdays and Sundays, and I teach them Bengali and Arabic' (p. 190). Children in the study who received no support of this kind from their mothers at home were sent to a tutor when they were eight years old. Literacy and schooling are often perceived as the route to social mobility in this and many other minority communities; parents therefore tend to be highly supportive.

Home-school reading schemes also highlight differences in expectations. Teachers usually assume that a parent – most often the mother – will listen to the child reading a book brought home from school for sharing. Yet in many communities older siblings and other family members play this role, particularly when parents do not speak the dominant language (Gregory, 1998; Kenner *et al.*, 2007). Parents often take a very different view of home-school reading initiatives. Some Bengali mothers express dissatisfaction with the frivolous nature of the material that children are asked to read; for them, stories are a vehicle for the teaching of moral principles. They also believe that it is the responsibility of the school and not the parents to teach their children to read (Gregory, 1996).

How do we explain differences in literacy achievement?

Limited access to officially sanctioned cultural knowledge clearly disadvantages some groups of children. Masny and Ghahremani-Ghajar (1999: 89) give several examples of the difficulties experienced by Somali elementary school children when doing exercises on inferencing and reading comprehension. The textbook answer of why parents might eat by candlelight was a power cut; Jamila, however, suggested that they would not want to disturb the children sleeping nearby. She also suggested that the police were chasing a car because they wanted to check if someone was hiding in the trunk, while the textbook explanation was that it might have driven through a red light.

One attempt to address differences of the kind observed for Jamila is Hirsch's (1987) theory of cultural literacy which proposes that, if some groups of children lack the background information and linguistic conventions required for effective reading and writing, then they should be taught explicitly 'the idioms, allusions and informal content of the dominant culture, from street signs to historical references'. It is doubtful whether the acquisition of a specific body of knowledge can ever be enough to achieve this end; equally important, it begs the question of *whose* knowledge is entailed. This approach is grounded in a deficit view which places the responsibility for underperformance on children and their families.

Increasingly, however, the focus is shifting to the school. Bourdieu's (1991, 1997) sociology of language and power (first mentioned in Chapter 3) provides a useful framework for understanding educational inequalities. He explains patterns of student performance in terms of the uneven distribution of three kinds of 'capital' – economic, social and cultural.

Economic capital can take the form, for instance, of paying for private schooling. *Social* capital, in the form of membership of a particular club or community, can facilitate access to privileged educational pathways. *Cultural* capital takes the form of favored 'ways of knowing and being'. Families with the right kind of capital are able to achieve the best outcomes for their children. The greater synergy between the experience of children from middle-class families and the norms and values of the school means that they experience far less disjuncture than children with different values and assumptions.

The initial focus for Bourdieu was social class. His framework has, however, been extended to include ethnicity and language. Blackledge's (2001) study of Bangladeshi women, for instance, shows how mothers with better developed skills in English who are more knowledgeable about British education have easier access to the 'dominant market': they receive more advice on how to support their children's reading than mothers less fluent in English and less familiar with the system. In acting in this way, the teachers were, of course, in danger of increasing inequality by excluding families in greatest need of support.

Case study: Troy and Abdul Rahman

Liz Brooker's (2002) case study of two five-year-old boys born on the same day – Abdul Rahman, a Bengali-heritage boy and Troy, his working-class English classmate – provides an excellent example of how the different capital of the families in question provides different outcomes for the children. There was little common ground in the attitudes towards literacy of the two families. Troy's parents felt that reading was a chore and his mother was of the view that words were to be learned and not guessed at. The approach of Abdul Rahman's parents was very different: they taught him, rhymes, letters and numbers and their daily routines demonstrated the uses of literacy and the value they attached to it.

Given the importance attributed by schools to participation in everyday literacy practices (such as making shopping lists or writing notes), it might be predicted that Rahman would make more rapid progress. In actual fact it was Troy – and not Rahman – who was taking off as a reader by the end of the first year in school. When we look closely at patterns of interaction between parents and teachers and at the experiences of the children in the classroom we begin to understand why this might be the case.

On starting school, Troy found himself at an advantage. He was familiar with the toys, equipment and activities; he knew culturally appropriate strategies for making friends with children; and he demanded high levels of interaction with adults. His parents shared information with the school about family life (the mother's pregnancy, family trips, home practices and pedagogy, and their son's achievements). Because, she made constant requests for information about his teaching and learning, his mother was rapidly inducted into the school approach to literacy learning. At the end of the first year, he was taking off in his reading and had been assigned to the 'top group'.

Rahman, in contrast, took time to settle. He made friends with other Bangladeshi boys but had few English-speaking friends. He demanded very little adult interaction and waited to be spoken to. His parents exchanged no information with teachers, who knew nothing of his mother's pregnancy, illness and bereavement or of their home practices and pedagogy. His mother, for her part, remained ignorant of the school's approach to literacy learning; she was, for instance, unaware that she was allowed to write on the home-school reading record in Bengali. At the end of the first year in school, Rahman had been assigned to the middle group.

While neither of these children conformed to the middle-class norms of the school, Troy's home experience provided greater continuity with school. His mother's regular communication with teachers helped to overcome early concerns about books and reading. The lack of communication between school and parents in the case of Rahman contributed to his lower position in the school hierarchy.

How have parents reacted?

In the absence of support for minority language use and literacy practices in mainstream schools, the only alternative open to minority families is to organize their own provision. It would seem that there are two main motives for this course of action: the first concerns the parents' desire to maintain the home language and culture; the second is dissatisfaction with mainstream schooling.

Literacy is inextricably linked in the Chinese diaspora with the transmission of traditional cultural beliefs, values and norms as witnessed not only by the widespread networks of community-based classes but also by accounts of the ways in which children's literacy learning is supported in the home (An Ran, 2000). Similarly, Bangladeshi children learn to read and write Bengali in order to gain access to a cultural world for which their grandparents fought during the struggle for independence from Pakistan in 1971. For the Bengali women in London interviewed by Blackledge (2001), learning to read and write Bengali was to be Bengali.

Concern over the quality of children's experience in mainstream schooling has also acted as a catalyst for many minority communities to explore alternative provision. Stokes (2000) identifies the increasing numbers of exclusions from schools as an indicator of the disaffection of the children. As one Somali parent commented: 'To be honest, I don't know why we bother to send our children to school' (p. 18). Gregory (1993) describes the distress of a Chinese grandfather at what he feels are the low expectations of the school. Coming from a tradition where great importance is attached to accuracy, he points to a drawing which has been labeled 'ToNy' and expresses his exasperation that his grandson cannot even write his name correctly.

Hornberger (2000: 356) describes community provision as 'an avenue for cultural expression' and 'a door of opportunity for the disempowered'. Gurnah (2001: 244) talks in terms of 'the affirmation of distinctive cultural identities and ... the building of learners' self-confidence'. Such developments are not, of course, of recent provenance. US Chinese language schools date back to 1848, when classes in Cantonese were organized for the residents of Chinatown in several large US cities (Chao, 1997). Religious institutions – the church, the mosque, the temple – have frequently played a vital role; overseas governments have also taken a lead. Traditionally, new arrivals were faced with two stark options: assimilate to the dominant group; or maintain heritage languages quietly at home and within the immediate ethnic community. The increasing demographic and economic strength of minorities has cleared the way for other courses of action. About half of the provinces of Canada now have heritage language programs in their official school curricula, most of which are delivered either on Saturdays or late afternoons in schools or in the community. Federal and state governments in Australia also offer students support through Saturday Schools when no classes are available at their own school in the form of free access to school buildings and professional development opportunities for teachers. In the UK, a recent survey found over 60 different languages taught to children after school or at weekends at 'complementary schools' or centers run by the communities themselves (CILT, 2005).

Two recent developments in the teaching of community or heritage languages are noteworthy. The first concerns increased cooperation between the different minorities: Community Languages Australia provides a meeting point for the ethnic schools of Australia; the National Resource Centre for Supplementary Education offers information, advice and resources for voluntary provision across England; the focus for the US National Heritage Language Resource Center is curriculum design, materials development and teacher education. The second development concerns the softening of attitudes on the part of mainstream educators towards the teaching of minority languages. Official support in Canada and Australia has been in evidence for several decades and more positive policies are also beginning to emerge in the US (Kagan *et al.*, 2007) and the UK (Edwards, 2008b).

These examples of minority provision both in and out of school reflect the growing political power of minority communities in countries of mass migration such as the US, Canada, the UK and Australia. In developing countries, other 'ruling passions', such as food shortages and high levels of disease and morbidity, inevitably take priority.

Case study: Ruling passions in Zimbabwe

Marriote Ngwaru (2008) set out to explore the interplay between the literacy at home and in school in rural Zimbabwe. He found, however, that parents wanted to raise other more pressing concerns before settling to talk about their children's schoolwork. As Mr Mhosva explained: 'I know you want us to talk about the education of our children but you will appreciate why we want to tell you about our problems so that at least you know the challenges we face everyday'.

The issue of food insecurity was one of the main ruling passions; virtually all families recounted anxieties about the vagaries of weather, shortage of farming inputs such as fertilizers and hybrid seed, and sometimes their own shortcomings as farmers. The families were hugely disadvantaged because they had no source of regular income and the crops they harvested were only sufficient for their own consumption.

Poor food security has implications for families' ability to deal with health issues. Members of the case study families suffered from a wide range of ailments and serious illnesses. Mbuya Nenji had just recovered from a life-threatening stroke, while other participants lived in the shadow of AIDS. Masona's eight-year-old daughter had been too ill to go to school for some time. His 15-year-old son was being treated for malaria at the local clinic and his daughter-in-law was lying in the sun looking very unwell. Funerals were commonplace, with the attendant financial worries. Political insecurity contributed still further to the anxieties of the families.

> The desire to be a good provider united all the families. Mbuya Pfunhu had 'one wish for these children, which is to provide enough resources to feed them clothe them and ensure that the young ones go to school'. Given these circumstances, the strongest of the ruling passions is understandably despair; literacy is a low priority for parents.

How do children reconcile home and school?

How, then, do children negotiate a route between the sometimes very different approaches to literacy at home and in school? And what room is there for negotiation between parents and teachers?

The extent of difference in teaching style between community and mainstream provision varies not only from one language group to another but also within the same group. Robertson (2006) sensitively draws attention to the different starting points and assumptions of teachers of children who speak Pahari, one of the languages of Pakistan, in three different settings – the mainstream classroom, a lunchtime class teaching Urdu the official language of Pakistan and after-school Qu'rānic classes. The mainstream teacher offers an 'English-Only' version of literacy where there is no space to explore children's prior knowledge and understanding of other languages. The teacher in the lunchtime Urdu club, in contrast, uses the children's bilingualism as a springboard for teaching and learning a third language, Urdu. Qu'rānic classes illustrate another approach to teaching and learning: here the children are given considerable autonomy in managing their individual learning.

The children's experience of literacy learning in three languages and of three pedagogical styles allows them to see literacies as systems. Far from perceiving these differences as confusing, they serve as a catalyst for thinking more deeply about reading and writing. Among the first things that children learn is procedural knowledge: what gets taught, when and how. In English classes, this may take the form of 'doing the title' before starting to read a book and, in Qu'rānic lessons, reciting by heart. They have a well-developed idea of 'how you do it properly' in each setting: they are eager, for instance, to explain that when they recite the Qu'rān, there should be 'no cheating'.

Kelly *et al.* (2001: 20) summarize the ways in which the experiences of Bangladeshi children differ from those of their monolingual peers:

> First, it is conducted as group rather than individual or paired activities, and an individual's progress (towards the completion of the Qu'rān for example) is often marked by the whole group sharing sweets or other treats. Second, the purpose of reading is quite different from that of monolingual English children: ... learning to read the Qu'rān is necessary for taking on the Islamic faith and therefore an adult and serious occupation. Finally, even the task of reading at home in English is quite different for Bangladeshi British children. In this community where some parents are literate in Bengali but not

necessarily in English, home reading usually means children reading their school texts not with Mum or Dad nor even with Grandma or Grandpa, but with those members of the family who are already fully proficient in English, i.e. the older sisters and brothers.

Gregory (1998) has shown how exposure to learning in a range of situations has allowed Bangladeshi children to develop 'syncretic literacy' where the repetition and fast pace of Qu'rānic reading coexist with strategies from mainstream schooling such as the 'chunking' of expressions and prediction. Older siblings provide scaffolding finely tuned to the needs of younger children. Initially, the more experienced readers provide almost every word; over time, the scaffolding is gradually reduced until the younger sibling is reading independently. It is possible to discern five separate stages in this development:

Listen and repeat: the child repeats word by word after the older sibling.
Tandem reading: the child echoes the sibling's reading, sometimes managing telegraphic speech.
Chained reading: the sibling begins to read and the child continues, reading the next few words until they need help again.
Almost alone: the child initiates reading and reads until a word is unknown; the sibling corrects the error or supplies the word; the child repeats the word correctly and continues.
The recital: the child recites the complete piece.

Case study: Learning to read the Qu'rān

The style of teaching in some community settings is very different from that in mainstream schools. In Qu'rānic classes, for instance, the teacher typically reads a phrase which the children then repeat until they are word perfect and move on to the next phrase. Field notes reproduced below from Rashid (cited in Kelly *et al.*, 2001: 18–19) give a flavor of this style of teaching.

In this particular class there are two male teachers, one of whom is working with the more advanced children who are tackling the complicated word structures of the Qu'rān. The other group consists of younger children who are in a different part of the room with the second teacher, grappling with sounds and letters and oral verse. Everyone sits on the mat swaying to the sound of their own voice. Although on initial appraisal the noise level seems high, little of this is idle chatter. It is the expressed wish of the teachers that children read aloud, partly to assist their learning, but more importantly so that Allah can hear. Children are encouraged to develop a harmonious recitation in unison with the gentle rocking to and fro which accompanies the reading. They are told that Allah listens to his servants and is pleased if they take time to make their reading meaningful...'Now, repeat after me', the teacher requests, 'Kalimah Tayyabh, la ilaha ilallaho, mohammadan rasolallahe'. He tells them to look at him as they repeat... I leave the room on the third recitation of the prayer and notice that the children have not wavered: all remain seated on the floor as they have done for the last hour and a half.

The teacher stands in the center and calls upon each child in turn to recite the passage which they have reached in their reading of the religious primer or the Qu'rān.

Teacher: Read this, Shuma

Shuma: Alif, bah, tah, sayh, (the names of the graphic symbols on the page)

Teacher: What was that? Say it again

Shuma:	Alif, bah, tah, sayh, jim
Teacher:	Yes, that's it, now carry on
Shuma:	Jim – jim, hae, kae, d- (hesitates)
Teacher:	Dal – dal, remember it and repeat
Shuma:	Dal, zal, rae, zae, sin, shin, swad, dwad,
Teacher:	(nods) What's next? Thoy, zoy
Shuma:	Zoy, thoy..
Teacher:	No, no, listen carefully. Thoy, zoy
Shuma:	(repeats)
Teacher:	Fine, now say it again from the beginning...

The work of Eve Gregory and her colleagues with the Bangladeshi community and of Leena Robertson with the Pihari community documents how children make meaning of contrasting literacy experiences. Teachers who ignore what happens at home and in the community are clearly failing to recognize the treasure trove available for school learning.

An Ran (2001) suggests that there are opportunities for far greater dialogue with parents and community leaders. In an analysis of four teacher–parent interviews involving Chinese families and interview data gathered before and after the meetings, she draws attention to important differences in orientation. The teachers tend to see learning as a developmental process and are happy with evidence that children are making progress towards a target. They tend to stress the positive aspects of children's achievements, evaluating their work as 'very good', 'good' and 'satisfactory'. Chinese parents, in contrast, are anxious to identify their children's weaknesses and push them to practice and improve; they therefore feel that teachers' evaluations are unrealistic and unhelpful. The teachers, for their part, perceive the parents' approach as unnecessarily harsh and undermining of children's confidence. Neither side seems to realize that the teachers' use of 'targets' and the parents' use of 'weaknesses' are essentially two sides of the same coin.

How can schools best support children's literacies?

All of the examples we have looked at in this chapter illustrate the very strong connections between language, literacy and power, first raised in Chapter 4. The unmistakable conclusion is that the ways of 'doing literacy' associated with some groups of children have greater resonance with teachers. Children whose ways of knowing and being match the expectations of the school are likely to experience less disjuncture and achieve better educational outcomes. In order to break this vicious cycle, the assumptions of both teachers and children need to be challenged. Various models of critical pedagogy have been developed to this end.

Critical literacy encourages students to question and challenge dominant beliefs and practices. Paulo Freire's (1970) *Pedagogy of the Oppressed,* for example, argues against the notion of students as empty vessels to be filled by the teacher and in favor of dialogue and open communication among students and teachers. He proposes that learners need to develop critical consciousness in order to recognize connections between their individual problems and experiences and the social contexts of which they are a part. Coming to consciousness is the first step in an ongoing, reflective approach to taking action to improve one's situation. More recently, Giroux's (1992) pedagogy of difference has focused on the ways in which schools mediate through both overt and hidden curricula that privilege some groups at the expense of others.

One obvious way forward is to incorporate home and other influences on students' culture, frequently ignored by teachers, into classroom learning. The work of Louis Moll and his associates on 'funds of knowledge' – the skills, ideas, practices and bodies of knowledge essential to the smooth running and well-being of a household – offers a clear model of the transformative potential of this approach (González *et al.,* 2005). Researchers and teacher researchers use visits to students' homes as the starting point for reflecting on their practice. The aim is to identify and document funds of knowledge. In Mexican families in Arizona, these funds of knowledge included farming and animal husbandry, construction, business and finance, household management, medicine and religion. They also looked at the social networks of relatives, friends and neighbors which allow for an exchange of these funds of knowledge, creating in the process *confianza*, or mutual trust.

Case study: Using children's funds of knowledge

The work of Moll and his associates contains many examples of how teachers were able to make links between the students' funds of knowledge. Most of Hilda's sixth grade bilingual students, for instance, were very reluctant learners, especially when it came to writing. Knowing that her students, their families and many other people in the community were knowledgeable about construction, she took a risk and developed a learning unit on the topic, although she knew nothing about construction herself.

Students were asked to do research on building, using books and magazines, before making model buildings for their homework project. Hilda invited parents and other members of the community with experience of construction to share their expertise and, by the end of the semester, 20 people had visited the class. Among the reading and writing activities the students undertook were short essays in either English or Spanish explaining their research, ideas and conclusions and a follow-up project requiring additional research which was written up in English and Spanish with the assistance of peer-editing groups.

Another teacher used a student's experiences of selling candy from Mexico in the United States to create a series of interdisciplinary lessons around candy production. She invited a parent who knew how to make Mexican candy to explain the process to the class and help them make their own candy. By the end of the week, the class had studied math concepts (e.g. average number of ingredients in US candy compared to Mexican candy), science concepts (e.g. chemical content of candy), health concepts (nutrition), consumer education (how to choose which candy is best), cross-cultural practices in the production of candy, marketing and advertising (e.g. how to price their own candy) and food production.

Cummins (2001) also attaches considerable importance to transformative pedagogy and points to a number of conditions likely to lead to more favorable educational outcomes. He argues that the incorporation of the language and culture of the community in the school will increase the self-esteem and emotional well-being of students. Equally important, the active involvement of families and the community in the education of their children will challenge negative views of minority communities. A further requirement is that teaching style should be both interactive and reciprocal. This approach gives students greater control over their learning and leads to enhanced self-esteem, greater cooperation and increased motivation. Finally, assessment should attempt, wherever possible, to locate problems in the social, economic or education system rather than assuming blame lies with the student.

Educational policy and practice tends to privilege one end of the continua of biliteracy discussed in Chapter 4. More prestige is attached, for instance, to written over oral development and to content in majority rather than minority languages. It is possible to argue, however, that by paying greater attention to the less powerful ends of the continua, educators, researchers, community members and policymakers will be better equipped to transform existing power structures. Teachers working in multilingual classrooms are well placed to help their students understand that the values associated with particular languages varieties are socially and culturally constructed, not fixed. In this way, students are empowered to see themselves not as the passive recipients but as people with the potential to make a difference.

Both of the case studies below demonstrate how this can work in practice. In the first, Nancy Hornberger and Ellen Skilton-Sylvester (2003) use two South American teacher narratives to show how teachers contest dominant discourse practices by encouraging the use of language and content traditionally excluded from the school. In the second (Cummins *et al.*, 2005), Canadian teachers and researchers – Jim Cummins, Vicki Bismilla, Patricia Chow, Sarah Cohen, Frances Giampapa, Lisa Leoni, Perminder Sandhu and Padma Sastri – explore the potential of *identity texts,* which encourage transfer of knowledge and skills across languages.

Case study: Some South American experiences

Early in her career, a Bolivian teacher of English and Quechua, Julia Pino Quispe, was assigned to a school in a mining center. Upon her arrival on the 1 May, the director told her that one of her responsibilities was to organize the annual celebration of Mothers' Day later that month. She worked hard and organized 'dances, funny toys, presents for the mothers, and other activities'; but what stands out most in her memory of that event is:

a girl who was frequently marginalised in her class because she was of peasant origin and this was still noticeable in her speech; and she offered to participate with a poem in Quechua which told of someone who had lost her mother and could not be consoled in her grief. The poem, of course, made the greatest impression and all were astonished because the form in which she interpreted the poem in Quechua could not have provided more originality nor more sense of life to all those who had the good fortune to be present. After this event, the girl was no longer excluded from any group; on the contrary it served to enable her to value her capacity to be included and it also served as a good example to her classmates.

In a similar vein, Concepción Anta tells of her work in an urban secondary school in Cajamarca where she finds that using local materials and natural resources enables her to work successfully with her students, who come from the outskirts of the city and are of very limited economic means.

> In a language class, where I am working with stories, I prefer to choose a peasant story, from a district or province of Cajamarca, worthy material from the locality, rather than choose a foreign story. First, I tell them the story and then with them we proceed to dramatize the story, using local materials from their own area; and finally with them we select some music to make a song from the story; this is something which they find very entertaining ... what I seek is for all aspects of the student or the person to continue functioning always as an integrated whole ... where man's lived experience is in conjunction with the life of the animals, the plants, the hills, the cliffs, the rivers, the stars, the fields, etc.

Both these examples – teacher Julia and the little girl who performs a poem in Quechua, and teacher Concepción and her class performing a local peasant story with local materials and local music – make use, in school contexts, of language and content which have historically been excluded from the school; they represent micro-level contestation of dominant discourse practices.

Case study: Dual language identity texts

When Madiha was in seventh grade — and less than a year after arriving in Canada — she co-authored a 20-page English-Urdu dual language book titled *The New Country* (see Figure 6.1). Together with her friends, Kanta and Sulmana, who had come from Pakistan three years before, she wrote about 'how hard it was to leave our country and come to a new country.'

The students researched and wrote the story over the course of several weeks, as part of a social studies unit on migration. Madiha spoke little English but was fluent in Urdu; Sulmana was fluent and literate in both Urdu and English; Kanta, who was fluent in Punjabi and English, had mostly learned Urdu in Toronto. The girls discussed their ideas primarily in Urdu but wrote the initial draft of their story in English. Sulmana served as scribe for both languages. The teacher researchers reflected on this experience thus:

> In a 'normal' classroom, Madiha's minimal knowledge of English would have severely limited her ability to participate in a 7th grade social studies unit. She certainly would not have been in a position to communicate extensively in English about her experiences, ideas, and insights. When the social structure of the classroom changed in simple ways, however, Madiha could express herself in ways that few English language learners experience in school. Her home language, in which all her experience prior to immigration was encoded, became once again a tool for learning. She contributed her ideas and experiences to the story, participated in discussions about how to translate vocabulary and expressions from Urdu to English and from English to Urdu, and shared in the affirmation that all three students experienced when they published their story.

> Students can create identity texts on any topic relevant to their lives or of interest to them. Sometimes teachers will suggest topics or ways of carrying out the project; in other cases, students will generate topics themselves and decide what form the projects will take. Because these projects require substantial time to complete, it is useful to aim for cross-curricular integration. That way, the project can meet standards in several different content areas. For example, students might research the social history of their communities through document analysis and interviews with community members. Such a project would integrate curricular standards in language arts, social studies, and technology.

Because students want to do the work in the first place, they generally treasure the product they have created and wish to share it with those they care about. This usually doesn't happen with worksheets, regardless of how accurately the student completes them. The worksheet has no life beyond its immediate function, whereas the identity text lives on for a considerable time, either in tangible form, as in a book, or as a digital text on the Web.

Figure 6.1 *The New Country* identity text

Key points

- Since the 1980s there has been a marked a shift in the conceptualization of literacy from a neutral to a political activity and the focus is now on what people *do with* literacy, rather than on what literacy can *do for* people.

- The new agenda of researchers is not, however, reflected in what is happening in schools where children's prior knowledge and learning are often marginalized. Many educators have little knowledge of children's experiences outside school and working-class and ethnic minority parents are often portrayed as not valuing literacy, even when this is patently not the case. Teachers also underestimate the role of siblings, grandparents and other family members in children's literacy learning.

- Traditionally, responsibility for underperformance has been attributed to the inadequacies of the home. The focus is, however, shifting. Bourdieu's sociology of

Language and Power explains patterns of student performance in terms of the uneven distribution of three kinds of 'capital' – economic, social and cultural. The values and assumptions of children from the dominant social group are much closer to those of the school than those of children from minority families, ensuring that they are perceived more favorably and receive more support.

- In the absence of support for minority language use and literacy practices in mainstream schools, minority families have no alternative but to organize their own provision. As the political power of minorities has grown, pressure has increased for governments to provide support for community.

- provision and also for the incorporation of minority language and literacy teaching in mainstream provision.

- Children have a well-developed idea of how you 'do literacy' in different settings and draw on elements of both community and school approaches in their own engagement with the written word. Teachers unaware of what happens outside the classroom are clearly unable to exploit these resources in school learning.

- Literacy is a social issue linked to class, gender and race oppression. Transformative pedagogy, however, offers a possible way of improving educational outcomes by encouraging students to question dominant beliefs and practices and by using language and content traditionally excluded from the school.

Activities and discussion points

1. Read the two extracts of conversations (taken from Freebody, 2001) where a researcher questions two teachers about how they would characterize the literacy experiences of working-class and middle-class children.

    How do you explain the different 'takes' on print in the environment?

    Extract 1: Working-class literacy

    t: ... they do basic functional reading and writing.

    r: What do you mean by functional?

    t: Enough to get them through the day. They can read the street signs. They can read the K Mart sign, they can read, ahh, well they can identify the signs.

    r: What about junk mail, catalogues?

    t: Well they can identify those because they are presented in a predictable text. So that they would probably understand them more than say a novel or that mixed structure of reading and then of course you know the children don't see that at home so they come to school wondering what all the hooha is about books.

Extract 2: Middle-class literacy

r: ... in the middle class homes where reading is valued, it's modelled, stories are read to them, the parents read, there are books around the house, the kids are, you know I think of the little ones who try to read the street signs and the labels at the Supermarket and things like that know what writing is....

2. If you come are literate in a minority language, reflect on ways in which your experiences of the written word at home and in the community contrast with how you learned in mainstream schooling.

3. If your own experience of reading and writing is limited to the dominant language, interview someone you know who has learned to read and write a minority language at home or in the community about how this differed from school learning.

Further reading

'Other' literacies

Gregory, E. & Williams, A. (2000) *City Literacies: Learning to Read Across Generations and Cultures.* London: Routledge.

Gregory, E., Long, S. & Volk, D. (2004) *Many Pathways to Literacy: Young Children Learning with Siblings, Grandparents, Peers and Communities.* London: Routledge.

Heath, S.B. (1983) *Ways with Words: Language, Life and Work in Communities and Classrooms.* Cambridge: Cambridge University Press.

Rosowsky, A. (2008) *Heavenly Readings: Liturgical Literacy in a Multilingual Context.* Clevedon: Multilingual Matters.

Wagner, D. (1993) *Literacy, culture and development:* Becoming literate in Morocco. Cambridge: Cambridge University Press.

Literacy learning in the community

Creese, A. & Martin, P. (eds) (2006) *Interaction in Complementary School Contexts: Developing Identities of Choice.* Special issue of *Language and Education* 20 (1).

Kagan, O., Bauckus, S. & Brinton, D. (eds) (2007) *Heritage Language Education: A New Field Emerging.* Mahwah, NJ: Lawrence Erlbaum.

Clyne, M. (1991) *Community Languages: The Australian Experience.* Cambridge: Cambridge University Press.

Community Languages Australia: www.communitylanguagesaustralia.org.au An umbrella body designed to unite the ethnic schools of Australia, and the state-based bodies which serve as their administrators.

National Resource Centre for Supplementary Education: www.continyou.org.uk/what_we_do/children_and_young_people/supplementary_education An organization dedicated to providing information, advice and resources to community or supplementary schools across England.

The National Heritage Language Resource Center: www.international.ucla.edu/languages/nhlrc Aims to develop effective pedagogical approaches to teaching heritage language learners, first by creating a research base and then by pursuing curriculum design, materials development and teacher education.

Transformative pedagogy

Cummins, J. (2001) *Negotiating Identities: Education for Empowerment in a Diverse Society.* Ontario, CA: California Association for Bilingual Education.

González, N., Moll, L. & Amanti, C. (eds) (2005) *Funds of Knowledge: Theorizing Practices in Households and Classrooms.* Mahwah, NJ: Lawrence Erlbaum.

7

Resources for learning

In this chapter we look at:

- The shortage of teaching and learning materials suitable for use in multilingual settings.

- The main kinds of learning materials currently available – textbooks, written with a specific pedagogical purpose and 'real books', designed for enjoyment.

- Innovative developments which make multilingual materials available in classrooms, including dual language texts, the multivariety approach, multimedia resources and self-made materials.

- The economics of minority language publishing: how centralized support and co-publishing initiatives can increase the flow of materials in other languages.

The shortage of materials

The shortage of suitable teaching materials is a problem for literacy teaching in multilingual settings of all kinds (Michael, 1989). The particular challenges however, vary from one situation to the next.

In the case of Indigenous and established languages, such as Irish and Frisian, the small numbers of speakers mean that print runs are uneconomical. This, in turn, limits the range and quality of materials (Edwards, 2008a).

Speakers of new minority languages potentially have access to books from the home country. Very often, however, imported materials fail to speak to the experience of locally born children and the linguistic level for any given age range is too advanced (MRC, 1995). As a result teachers have to spend a great deal of time in lesson preparation and the production of resources. In some cases, differences in the quality of color reproduction or paper, may make materials produced abroad less attractive to students than materials for the home market.

Sub-Saharan Africa faces yet another set of challenges (Edwards, 2008a). The lack of disposable income means that the education departments are the main market for books for children, the vast majority of which are written in former ex-colonial languages. There is a shortage of writers and editors able to work in African languages and of illustrators sensitive to African cultural content; there are also problems in distributing the books.

Kinds of resources

It is possible to distinguish two main kinds of learning materials. Of these, textbooks are widely regarded as the single most important instructional material. Other resources include 'real books' written for enjoyment rather than with a specific pedagogical purpose.

Textbooks

For students, textbooks – written with a specific pedagogical purpose – are a useful reference source; they can also be a resource for self-directed learning against which progress can be measured. From the perspective of teachers, textbooks save time in lesson preparation while, at the same time, allowing for adaptation and improvisation. Because they are produced in large quantities, they are relatively inexpensive and therefore cost-effective.

The main criticism of textbooks is that they privilege some aspects of culture over others. Luke (1988: 64) views textbooks 'as the interface between the officially state-adopted and sanctioned knowledge of the culture, and the learner' and as 'a specialised means for the ritual introduction of children into a culture's values and knowledge'. Apple (1988) argues in a similar vein that textbooks play a more important role in defining the curriculum than official curriculum statements. Analyses of content point consistently to the over-representation of whites, middle-class people, males and urban dwellers and to the relative invisibility of non-whites, working-class people, rural dwellers and the disabled (De Castell *et al.*, 1989; McKinney, 2005). In recognition of the importance of children being able to see themselves in the materials that they read, growing efforts are being made to redress these imbalances.

The role of the state in determining the version of history retold in textbooks has sometimes resulted in controversy. This was the case, for instance, in Japan where the government authorization system was criticized for rejecting textbooks that depict Imperial Japan in a negative way (Japan Times, 2007). The portrayal of Arabs in textbooks in the Jewish school system in Israel has also been the subject of critical scrutiny (Abu-Saad, 2007). Vested interest in textbooks, however, is not always ideological: sometimes the motive is financial. Richard Feynman's experience of sitting on a US commission to evaluate science textbooks included attempts at bribery (Feynman & Leighton, 1997). On one occasion, a textbook that contained blank pages received positive critiques.

Textbooks assume an even more important role in developing countries where learning materials are scarce and there are shortages of trained teachers. In these settings, the availability of textbooks has been shown to be the single most consistently positive school factor in predicting academic achievement (Henevald & Craig, 1996). Education policies in many developing countries are attaching growing importance to textbook provision. The Ghana Ministry of Education, for instance, finally fulfilled a long-standing promise in 2005 to provide all pupils in basic level education with a textbook for core subjects (Opoku-Amankwa, 2008).

Most of the work which highlights the importance of textbooks has been based on retrospective surveys and experimental studies. These offer limited information on either the interaction between pupils, teachers and the text or pupil access. In spite of the Ghanaian textbook policy, damage in transit, pilfering and problems of storage may prevent books reaching schools; teachers threatened with surcharges for lost and damaged books may be reluctant to distribute them to pupils. Kwasi Opoku-Amankwa (2008) describes some of these classroom realities.

Case study: Textbooks in Miss Akua's class

The book to pupil ratio in Mrs Akua's class is 1:3 in spite of the fact there are enough textbooks in the three core subjects for each student to have their own copy. The official policy also recommends that pupils be allowed to take their textbooks home. Again, this seldom if ever happens in practice because books for lower primary classes can only be replaced after three years and for upper primary classes after four years and teachers are afraid that the children will lose or damage them.

The main reasons offered by Mrs Akua for not following government policy, however, were the large class sizes and the seating arrangements in the classrooms. With 60 or more students and only 20 desks, the pupils sit three to a desk. The textbook is 8.5 inches by 10.5 inches in size; when open, two books take up the entire surface of the desk. The class teacher expects one book to be centrally placed on the desk so as to ensure each student has access, but 'fair use' rarely occurs.

The position of the book is largely determined by the political and social dynamics of the class. If the power broker sits in the middle, then the book is centrally placed for use by all the three students, though only the pupil seated in the middle has full access. The book was, however, rarely in the middle. If placed to the left or right, only one pupil had access; the other two were often observed dozing, chatting with friends and showing little interest in the class activity.

Reading schemes and basal readers

Basal readers (to use the American terminology) or reading schemes (the UK equivalent) are designed to offer children a carefully structured exposure to texts of increasing difficulty as they learn to read. Like other kinds of textbook, they have been the subject of much criticism.

Reading schemes are closely tied to particular approaches. In series such as *Dick and Jane* published in the US from the 1930s to the 1970s (or *Janet and John* and *Peter and Jane* in the UK), the focus was on word recognition and repetition (see Figure 7.1). When the *Dick and Jane* books were reissued in 2003 their nostalgic value ensured some 2.5 million sales. Significantly, however, the publishers warned against using them to teach reading to children.

Come, Dick.

Come and see.

Come, come.

Come and see.

Come and see Spot.

Look, Spot.

Oh, look.

Look and see.

Oh, see.

8

9

Figure 7.1 Spread from Fun with Dick and Jane (reissued by Grosset & Dunlap in 2007)

The task of weaving interesting stories from a limited set of words – in this case ones with predictable spellings – also proved a challenge for the programs influenced by the phonics-based approaches, which replaced them in the 1970s. These schemes, too, were criticized for focusing on the teaching of isolated skills, instead of fostering an enjoyment of reading for its own sake (Edwards, 1995). As whole language approaches to the teaching of reading gradually gained ground in the late 1980s, the focus shifted increasingly to real – or trade – books, rather than textbooks. More recently, the talents of successful children's authors have been used in creating authentic and enjoyable stories as part of reading schemes.

'Real books'

Particularly in the US, the UK, Australia and Aotearoa/New Zealand, the emphasis in the early stages since the early 1980s has been on reading for enjoyment, using 'real books' (sometimes also known as 'trade books') rather than textbooks, though real books are often used in parallel with basal readers or reading schemes. Even in Africa, where economic and other considerations have led to a heavy dependence on textbooks, there is a gradual move towards the use of 'supplementary reading material' (Rosenberg, 2000).

Reading for pleasure has been linked with high levels of reading attainment, writing ability, text comprehension, breadth of vocabulary and greater self-confidence in both first and second language readers (Clark & Rumbold, 2006). It has also been shown to increase general knowledge and understanding of other cultures and to provide a greater insight into human nature and decision-making (Häggsblom, 2006). Identified as more important for children's educational success than the socio-economic status of their family (OECD, 2002), reading for pleasure is seen by some as an important factor in combating social exclusion.

Individual real books reflect the same range of bias as textbooks; collectively they offer access to a much wider range of experience. They are, however, less cost-effective than textbooks, which are produced in much larger numbers.

Innovative approaches

Educational materials have traditionally been based on the standard language. In many cases, they are commissioned and regulated by government and, as such, serve as an important tool in both the exclusion of large numbers of children who speak non-standard varieties and in consolidating the advantages of standard speakers. Further, the monolingual materials which form the staple diet of most schoolchildren conspicuously fail to build on bilingual learners' personal resources. In contrast, each of the initiatives described below – dual language books, the multivariety approach, multilingual multimedia and self-made materials – attempts to redress this imbalance.

Dual language books

Dual language books first appeared in the 1980s in response to this perceived need. Writers such as Feuverger (1994) and MRC (1995) draw attention to their usefulness in, on the one hand, supporting children's literacy development in two languages and, on the other hand, raising the cultural and linguistic awareness of *all* children. More recently, Sneddon (2008), reports on how two women and their children used both Albanian/English dual texts in transferring skills from one language to another and in negotiating meaning in both languages, as well as in comparing reading strategies.

Dual language publications usually take the form of children's picture books where the illustrations are accompanied by texts in two languages – one 'official', the other a minority language (see Figure 7.2).

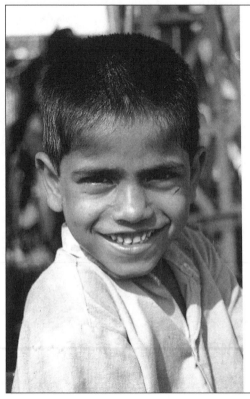

ਮੇਰਾ ਨਾਂ ਬਾਬੂ ਹੈ ਅਤੇ ਇਹ ਕਿਤਾਬ ਮੇਰੇ ਜੀਵਨ ਵਿਚੋਂ ਇਕ ਦਿਨ ਬਾਰੇ ਹੈ। ਮੈਂ ਬੰਬਈ ਦੇ ਬਾਹਰਲੇ ਇਲਾਕੇ ਵਿਚ ਆਪਣੇ ਮੰਮੀ, ਡੈਡੀ ਅਤੇ ਭੈਣਾ ਭਰਾਵਾਂ ਨਾਲ ਰਹਿੰਦਾ ਹਾਂ।

My name is Babu and this book is about a day in my life. I live on the outskirts of Bombay with my mum and dad, and my brothers and sisters.

Figure 7.2 A page from the Panjabi–English version of *Babu's Day* (Kapur, 1997)

Many monolingual English-speaking teachers welcomed dual texts enthusiastically as something new and different; minority language-speaking teachers have often felt more cautious. Some were unhappy with the variable quality of translation; others expressed concern that, as long as there was an English text, bilingual children would have little motivation to read the other language. In addition, there were issues of status: which language comes first? And in a book where one language runs from left to right and the other right to left, where does the book begin? There is evidence that details of this kind influence children's attitudes towards the languages in question, often negatively (MRC, 1995).

Yet the juxtaposition of languages opens up interesting pedagogical possibilities for even very young children. Discussion of differences in word order or the direction of different scripts leads to a greater awareness of language (Edwards *et al.*, 2000, 2002); it also encourages children to think about the nature of translation: are they aiming for word-for-word meaning or trying to communicate the sense of the first text in composing the second?

The presence of dual language books – and multilingual resources more generally – is, on some levels, largely symbolic since mere access to these resources does not ensure that minority language-speaking children become biliterate. Multilingual resources cannot simply be left to languish on shelves or computers: teachers need to bring them to the attention of their students and to explore ways of using these materials. Involving bilingual parents, children and members of the community is an important part of this process.

Nonetheless, resources of this kind send powerful messages to both speakers of minority languages and speakers of the dominant language about the status of other languages. And in the case of dual language books, children who speak only the dominant language are able to improve their knowledge about language, often by working collaboratively with minority language-speaking peers.

Multivariety approaches

Especially in countries where textbooks and other learning resources are commissioned and regulated by government, the choice is usually the standard national language. Traditionally, the focus has been on the development of pedagogies to help children acquire the standard language as the route to social mobility. Sometimes the aim has been to eliminate non-standard language taking a deficit approach. On other occasions, the aim has been to extend children's language repertoire rather than eliminate the non-standard variety. Ramírez *et al.*'s (2005) discussion of Ebonics debate in the US is a good example of this approach; so too is Sharifian *et al.*'s (2004) treatment of Australian Aboriginal English.

There is a danger, however, that attempts to teach a second dialect underestimate the complex interactions between language and identity. In the case study which follows, Busch and Schick (2006) take a radically different approach to dialect diversity in Bosnia Herzogovina. Although the varieties spoken in this region are mutually intelligible, language has been used across the various communities to emphasize differences. In Serbia, Cyrillic was adopted as the national script; in Croatia, dictionaries of Serbian words and their Croatian equivalents were published with the explicit aim of helping people demonstrate their national consciousness through language; in areas where Bosnians exercised political control, differences in orthography and a standard influenced by Turkish were emphasized.

Case study: Textbook development in Bosnia Herzogovina

In 1998 the Austrian NGO KulturKontakt Austria embarked on a project to develop supplementary teaching material for civic education in Bosnia Herzogovina. This led to the publication in 2001 of *Pogledi: Open teaching and intercultural learning*. A team of 25 teachers, teacher trainers, principals, academics and representatives of the NGO took part in a series of workshops to develop materials to be piloted in schools. The resulting publication consists of six teaching units targeted at students between the ages of 13 and 15.

Most other educational materials in the region are printed in separate Bosnian, Croatian and Serbian editions. In contrast, a single version of *Pogledi* now serves upper primary and secondary schools throughout Bosnia Herzegovina, as well as parts of the Federation and the Republika Srpska. This was achieved by assembling a range of materials, reproduced in their original form, including contemporary and historical literary texts, advertisements, leaflets and official publications to be used as a resource for students. Individual learners are thus able to find themselves and their linguistic practices in at least some of the texts. They also come to an appreciation that difference depends on a range of factors – in addition to ethnicity or nationality – and need not be an obstacle to understanding.

For these reasons, *Pogledi* should be viewed not simply as a celebration of diversity but as an educational project which is emancipatory in intent. A multivariety approach might be expected to meet with resistance because it challenges the status quo. Its success in a region which saw some of the most bitter conflict of the 20th century is therefore all the more remarkable. It has potential for use in a wide range of other complex situations, such as the teaching of Romany transnationally or of the closely related Nguni languages in Southern Africa.

Multimedia, multilingual materials

The immense flexibility of electronic resources means that there is no limit to the number of varieties that can be stored in terms of either text or audio. There is also no limit to the ways in which different varieties – or combinations – can be displayed, opening a range of possibilities for discussion of explicit differences between standard and non-standard varieties, or between one language and another. The main obstacles are economic and attitudinal. The focus in software development is inevitably market-driven, with solutions coming online more rapidly for languages spoken by the largest numbers of people. The availability of open source software and the growing expertise in ICT of minority language speakers will, of course, open up increasing opportunities for development in this area.

The move to web-based resources is much to be welcomed by those with easy access to broadband Internet. The quantity of multilingual web-based materials is growing. Considerable progress has been made, for instance, in providing support for the learning of Chinese characters on websites such as yellow bridge.com and zhongwen.com. The quality of electronic resources, however, remains variable. The addition of fresh content also remains a challenge for many languages. To give just one example, at the time of writing, no activities had been added in the previous two years to the 'fun and games' section of the excellent Twfcymru.com website, which promotes the benefits of bilingualism to parents. Yet without considerable investment in new material, there is little incentive for parents and their children to make return visits. For the time being, then, paper materials remain the most important and accessible resources for teaching and learning.

Self-made materials

Another solution to the dearth of reading materials in minority languages involves self-made materials which address the needs and interests of specific groups of children. This approach sits very comfortably with constructivist 'Whole Language' approaches which often use 'stories' dictated by children as reading materials in the early stages (Goodman, 2005). Because it is easy to predict what comes next, success in reading back the story builds confidence. And, as we saw in the discussion of identity texts in Chapter 6, it also works well with older children.

Teachers and parents can also usefully be involved in producing reading materials: their familiarity with the children's world and what interests them allows them to introduce themes and detail that children can identify with. Materials produced in this way can be highly motivating for all concerned, as illustrated in the following case study of Pakistani mothers producing stories in Urdu for their children.

Case study: Multilingual word processing in Urdu

The introduction of an Urdu word-processing program in Urdu in Redlands Primary School, where a significant number of children were of Pakistani heritage, made it possible to produce high quality materials for children. It also had a range of other – less expected – benefits.

An initial workshop, facilitated by two Pakistani teachers and attended by six mothers, provided hands-on experience of Urdu word-processing. In subsequent workshops, they went on to complete a range of simple stories for their children; two also volunteered to help with computer-based activities at a lunchtime Urdu club organized by one of the teachers. Most of the mothers spoke little English and had not previously taken part in school activities. The warm reception from the school sent valuable messages about the importance attached to linguistic and cultural diversity in learning.

The project also usefully challenged commonly held assumptions. Teachers were surprised to find that many more mothers than expected were able to read and write Urdu, that initial computer-phobia can be quickly overcome and that, given suitable encouragements, even very shy parents are happy to be involved in their children's schooling.

The children were clearly pleased at the expert help provided by their mothers. Following a school assembly when children described computer-based activities in Urdu club, the numbers of regular attendees grew rapidly from six to 22, a third of whom came from English-speaking families. Although the club had always theoretically been open to non-Pakistani heritage children, the uptake had previously been very limited. There were also reports of children helping each other to learn and practice Urdu in the playground.

The economics of minority language publishing

As we have seen, the shortage of good quality books for children is an ongoing challenge in many different multilingual settings. One way forward is by offering centralized support. The Welsh Book Council, for instance, provides specialist services for publishers in editing, design, marketing and distribution (Edwards, 2004). Another promising way forward involves co-publishing agreements – two or more publishers collaborate in the production of the same picture book, making it possible to increase the print run and reduce the unit price. The book passes through the presses four times, with the different language texts added in the final run. Thus the costs of printing, illustration and origination are shared. Both these developments have the potential to increase the amount of reading material in minority languages by making children's publishing economically viable.

The two case studies which follow show how co-publishing initiatives have made it possible to provide good quality books for children in a range of lesser-used European languages and African languages.

> **Case study:** *A Lovely Bunch of Coconuts*
>
> Fabula, a European Commission-funded project on multilingual, multimedia materials for children, provides a good example of how co-publishing can work in practice. The team began by identifying an existing children's book to be repurposed as a multimedia storybook. *A Lovely Bunch of Coconuts* (Reader, 1989) proved eminently suitable: its strong storyline and universal appeal made it an excellent exemplar multimedia story for use across Europe (see Figures 7.3) (Edwards *et al.*, 2000, 2002).
>
>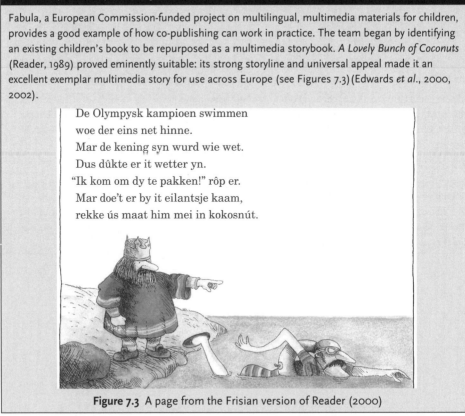
>
> **Figure 7.3** A page from the Frisian version of Reader (2000)

Having translated the English text into all the project languages the team worked with the original publisher and publishers in the partner countries on new versions of the book. Contracts were finally signed for 5000 copies of an English edition, 3000 copies in Welsh and Irish and 1000 copies in Basque, Frisian and Dutch. Serendipitously, South African associates found funding for a further 1000 copies in isiXhosa. With a print run of some 15,000 copies, the unit price was affordable for all concerned.

Case study: Stories across Africa

The same South African colleagues responsible for the isiXhosa version of *A Lovely Bunch of Coconuts* were involved in another co-publishing venture (Edwards, 2007b). PRAESA (The Project for the Study of Alternative Education) at the University of Cape Town is at the hub of *Stories Across Africa,* a pan-African project with two targets. One is to publish anthologies which will give children and caregivers across the continent the opportunity to read the same stories in their own languages and languages of wider communication. Stories old and new are being collected, written, rewritten, illustrated and translated into many different languages. The other target is a pan-African set of 16 *Little Hands* books for young children from birth to six years to celebrate the African Union Year of African Languages (see Figure 7.4).

Figure 7.4 Poster advertising *Little Hands* books

> The focus here is on good quality books that speak to the experience of young children and their families. Currently some 24 titles have been published in 24 languages. Brian Wafawarowa, the publisher for the *Little Hands* books in South Africa is clear about the advantages of this approach:
>
>> The unit price for South Africa is greatly reduced ... those outside get [the books] at a much lower price than they could on their own. Just to play with numbers a bit, I don't think a publisher in Ethiopia with a language like Tigrinya would be able to do 500 copies. But with our print run of say 20,000 the savings are massive. To take an example of a book we did earlier, the production costs were going to be 52 US cents. But when we brought in other countries we ended up with a cost of 28 US cents a book, which is a huge saving. We transferred these savings to the market not because we are philanthropic capitalists but because we have to make sure that the price you come up with is viable.

The co-publishing arrangements described in the case studies apply to established and African languages – two of the three categories discussed in Chapter 2. There is also potential to achieve economies of scale for the third category, new minority languages. Although national markets for dual language texts are relatively small, there are opportunities for extending markets, particularly in the English-speaking world. Thus books in English and Panjabi produced in the UK are potentially of interest to schools serving Panjabi speakers in the US, Canada and Australia. There are also opportunities for reducing costs. Using the same principles as those outlined above for *A Lovely Bunch of Coconuts* and the *Little Hands* books, publishers are able to produce different versions of the same picture book in several language combinations.

Key points

There is a dearth of teaching materials suitable for use in multilingual settings. The challenges include uneconomical print runs for small numbers of speakers of established languages; inappropriate content and linguistic level for speakers of new minority languages in materials imported from the country of origin; and lack of capacity and infrastructure in the production of African language materials.

There are two main kinds of learning materials: textbooks and supplementary reading material or 'real books'.

- While textbooks save time and are cost-effective, they often privilege some aspects of culture over others. Textbooks are closely tied to particular approaches to teaching, which may be less suited to bilingual readers.

- Real books are designed for enjoyment. Their use has been linked with high levels of reading attainment, writing ability, text comprehension, breadth of vocabulary and greater self-confidence in both first and second language readers. They are, however, less cost-effective than textbooks, which are produced in much large numbers.

Various initiatives in materials development are responding to linguistic diversity in innovative ways:

- Dual language books support bilingual children's literacy development in two languages at the same time as raising the cultural and linguistic awareness of *all* children.

- The multivariety approach uses a range of authentic materials, e.g. contemporary and historical literary texts, advertisements and leaflets, allowing individual learners to find themselves and their linguistic practices in at least some of the texts.

- Multilingual, multimedia materials offer immense flexibility: there is no limit to the number of varieties that can be stored in terms of either text or audio.

- Self-made materials involving teachers, parents and children use familiarity with the children's world and what interests them as a strong motivating force for reading and writing.

Economies of scale offer another way forward. Co-publishing agreements, where two or more publishers collaborate in the production of the same picture book, make it possible to increase the print run, and reduce the unit price. In the process, they increase the amount of reading material in minority languages by making children's publishing economically viable.

Activities and discussion points

1. Share your experiences of learning to read. To what extent did the books you use reflect the world that you were living in and why does this matter?

2. Using an Internet search engine, choose a particular minority language and explore which teaching and learning resources are available for children.

3. How can multilingual resources be used to best effect in the classroom? What pitfalls should be avoided?

Further reading

Textbooks

Luke, A. (1988) *Literacy, Textbooks, and Ideology*. London: Falmer Press.

McKinney, C. (2005) *Textbooks for Diverse Learners: A Critical Analysis of Learning Materials Used in South African Schools*. Cape Town: HSRC Press.

Real books

Clark, C. & Rumbold, K. (2006) *Reading for Pleasure: A Research Overview*. London: National Literacy Trust. Retrieved from: www.literacytrust.org.uk/Research/readpleasure.html.

Organisation for Economic Cooperation and Development (OECD) (2002) *Reading for Change: Performance and Engagement Across Countries. Results from PISA 2000*. New York: OECD.

Dual language books

Multilingual Resources for Children Project (MRC) (1995) *Building Bridges: Multilingual Resources for Children*. Clevedon: Multilingual Matters.

Edwards, V. & Walker, S. (1996) Some Status Issues in the Translation of Children's Books. *Journal of Multilingual and Multicultural Development* 17 (5): 339–48.

Using and Researching Dual Language Books for Children – A Resource for Teachers and Researchers: www.uel.ac.uk/education/research/duallanguagebooks

The multivariety approach

Busch, B. & Schick, J. (2006) Educational Materials Reflecting Heteroglossia: Disinventing Ethnolinguistic Differences in Bosnia-Herzegovina. In A. Pennycook & S. Makoni (eds) *Disinventing and Reinventing Language*. Clevedon: Multilingual Matters, pp. 216–32.

Multilingual wordprocessing

Edwards, V., Chana, U. & Walker, S. (1998) Hidden Resources: Multilingual Wordprocessing in the Primary School. *Race, Ethnicity and Education* 1 (1): 49–61.

The economics of minority language publishing

Edwards, V. (2007b) The Economics of Minority Languages: Promotion and Publishing. Paper presented at the 11th International Conference on Minority Languages, Pecs, Hungary, 5–7 July.

Edwards. V. (2008a) *An Evaluation of the Culture of Reading, a Core PRAESA Project*. Cape Town: PRAESA.

Electronic teaching and learning resources

Yellow Bridge: www.yellowbridge.com Provides animated stroke order information for Chinese characters.

Twf: www.twfcymru.com A website which promotes the benefits of bilingualism to parents and includes some language learning activities for children.

8

Making change in multilingual classrooms

This book has identified a range of challenges for literacy teaching and learning in multilingual settings. It has also discussed a number of ways in which schools can respond more effectively to children's needs. Making change, however, is not an easy process. This chapter:

■ sets out the urgent need for the continuing professional development (CPD) of teachers;

■ identifies the weaknesses of traditional models of delivery;

■ considers what effective professional development looks like, paying particular attention to the transformative potential of 'communities of practice' where people with a common interest collaborate over an extended period, to share ideas and solve problems, thus taking ownership of the change process;

■ emphasizes the role of international collaboration in finding solutions to common problems.

The need for training

Teachers working in multilingual communities frequently find themselves reinventing pedagogies devised originally with monolingual, more culturally homogenous populations in mind. They need to engage with a host of issues which vary from one setting to the next: in countries of immigration, are new arrivals best taught separately or in mainstream classrooms? Is phonics teaching suitable for children learning to read in English as an additional language? How much time needs to be dedicated in bilingual programs to each language? To what extent does this vary over time and from one setting to the next? These and a host of other questions confront teachers on a daily basis.

As answers to these questions have gradually become clearer, so, too, has the need for training. There are however, serious shortages of specialist second language teachers, bilingual educators and heritage/community language teachers. Competition for time in both initial teacher education and continuing professional development is intense, due in part, at least to the paradigm shift which has been taking place in education internationally. In the UK, for instance, primary school teachers have been required to develop a range of new competencies at the same time as implementing new assessment and recording procedures. These changes have taken place in a highly politicized and nationalistic framework which often overlooks the needs and experiences of minority groups (Soler, 2001). The 2002 *No Child Left Behind* legislation has given rise to a similar upheaval in the US (Crawford, 2008).

A considerable body of research points to the importance of leadership for improving educational outcomes (Gray *et al.*, 1999; Teddlie & Reynolds, 2000). Effective leaders have a strong sense of mission but, at the same time, encourage a participative approach. They focus on the importance of academic goals and processes and demonstrate a concern with pupil learning at the classroom level. They have a hands-on approach to the selection and replacement of teachers and the monitoring of staff performance. They also attach importance to monitoring and evaluating systems at the school level. Last but by no means least, they motivate staff to have high expectations of students. Effective leadership is also responsive to the different stages of a school's development: the emphasis on staff ownership of an initiative needs to increase in step with levels of competence as systems and practices improve. Continuing professional development (CPD) plays a central role in this process.

Approaches to continuing professional development

Teachers faced with an ever-expanding knowledge base need to update their skills and adapt to new roles and expectations throughout their careers, creating a need for continuing professional development (CPD). Currently, two competing discourses dictate the form of CPD: the teacher as 'technician' (based on the needs of institutions) and the teacher as 'reflective practitioner' (based on beliefs about the teacher as a person and professional) (Christie *et al.*, 2004; Stuart & Kunje, 2000). Those who subscribe to the 'teacher as technician' position tend to see CPD as a means of addressing defects, such as inefficiency and lack of training. Advocates of the 'teacher as reflective practitioner', in contrast, favor a growth approach, where the imperative is to develop creative responses to complex and ever-changing classroom realities.

Attempts to offer CPD which adopt a defect approach have attracted a wide range of criticisms (Guskey, 2000). All too often teachers are 'force fed' with information and more attention is paid to content than to learning processes. Few attempts are made to meet the needs of teachers with differing levels of experience. Initiatives are piecemeal and often take the form of a series of unrelated workshops with little follow-up or guidance on implementation. Equally worrying is the politically driven desire for quick results, reinforced in the case of *No Child Left Behind* in the US by the threat of penalties for schools unable to deliver. Where these criticisms are valid, it is unlikely that teacher practice will be effective or that student outcomes will improve.

The 'cascade' model of training, which is widely considered to be the most cost-effective method for large-scale training, suffers from many of these problems. This approach has been used in diverse contexts, including the implementation of the National Literacy Strategy in England. It usually starts by providing training for a relatively small number of specialists or trainers in the relevant knowledge and skills. Recipients of such 'first level' training are expected to train other groups (usually classroom teachers), and these teachers are then expected to share the information gathered from the training with their colleagues when they return to their schools. This model is particularly attractive to school administrators because it minimizes the problems of teacher absence.

Hayes (2000: 138) outlines five issues fundamental to the success of cascade training:

- the approach must be experiential and reflective;
- it must be open to reinterpretation – rigid adherence to prescribed ways of working should not be expected;
- expertise should be diffused as widely as possible, not concentrated at the top;
- a cross section of stakeholders must be involved in the preparation of training materials;
- decentralization of responsibilities is desirable.

The case study which follows is based on Shireena Basree bt Abdul Rahman's (2007) account of the training provided by the Malaysia Ministry of Education for an initiative to improve the standard of English teaching. Her experience suggests that, when these conditions are not in place, the outcomes are disappointing.

Case study: Contemporary Children's Literature Programme (CCL)

Training for CCL was provided first at the national level for the 'Main Trainers' who were responsible, in turn, for delivering training at the state level for one teacher working with the relevant grade from each school in the state. On completing the course, the teachers were expected to provide in-house training for other colleagues teaching English in their schools.

The Main Trainers expressed serious reservations about the usefulness of the state-level training they were providing. The national shortage of English teachers meant that they were often working instead with head teachers or even 'guru kursus' [teachers responsible for attending training courses of all kinds] with no experience of English teaching. On other occasions, they raised concerns about the limited teaching experience of course participants and whether they would be able to 'cascade' what they had been taught to colleagues responsible for the delivery of CCL in their schools.

The Main Trainers were also worried about whether in-house training was even taking place. This skepticism would appear to be justified: none of the teachers who participated in the study had received school-level training. In-house training, in general, appeared to be accorded low priority. Trainers reported that most teachers showed very little interest in the content and appeared more concerned with bringing the session to an end as quickly as possible:

> People will be worried about ... they have to go home, cook for their family, and how long is this teacher going to make us sit down and listen to all this, they will say... So, you [the trainer] will tend to rush through things. But that is the reality.

The evidence of classroom observation and interviews with head teachers, English teachers and children, was that the approach advocated in the CCL training was having very little impact on classroom practice.

So what does effective CPD look like?

We know what doesn't work. But equally important, a picture is emerging of what works best. Professional development needs to be driven by a clear idea of the goals to be achieved. It needs to be a systemic process: one-off workshops don't work because they fail to offer ongoing support for those charged with change or to involve all relevant members of the school community. Most important, professional development needs to be seen as an ongoing process: it is simply not enough to devote a few days a year to the current priority.

Researchers at the US Center for the Improvement of Early Reading Achievement (Taylor *et al.*, 2005) argue that, because it is a complex, year-on-year process, school improvement requires at least five or six years to fully appreciate the nature of the change. Researchers on the Secondary Schools Literacy Initiative (SLLI) in Aotearoa/New Zealand (see May & Smyth, 2007, and the case study below) also argue for the importance of seeing school change as a longer-term project and suggest that it takes at least three to five years of sustained engagement in a school to begin to have a significant impact on literacy outcomes. They point to three stages of change. In the initial phase, the aim is to raise staff awareness of the *need* for change over a period of time that varies according to the 'readiness' of the teachers to engage with the issues. In the second phase, the focus moves to *experimentation* with strategies and knowledge which research has demonstrated to be useful, and to developing the skills of self-reflection in collaboration with colleagues. In the final phase, the goal is to *sustain* changed practices over time.

From research to classroom practice

One of the quandaries faced by those of us trying to transform various aspects of education like literacy teaching, is that we have to grapple with how responsible adults – teacher trainers, teachers and, in some cases, parents – come to change their ideas and practice. It is not enough to be told *what* to do when you teach reading and writing, without understanding *why* this should be the case. Nor is being told *why* you should teach in a particular way sufficient if one is not able to engage with the ideas at a practical level. For shifts in practice to take place that reflect new understandings, people also need to know *how* to make changes concrete. My research experiences, informed by my role as a parent, a teacher and a teacher educator, suggest that this is a slow, cyclical process involving opportunities to observe reading and writing practice, reflect and discuss, read related contesting views and theories, reflect on these, try out adjusted practice based on fresh insights, with guidance from and interaction with a more experienced 'other'. (Bloch, 2007: 7)

As Carole Bloch points out, changing teacher practice is a complex process which requires careful consideration of *what, why* and *how*. The *what* and *why* of professional development are perhaps the least urgent considerations: although much remains to be discovered, we have a reasonably clear of what works best, underpinned by theoretical understandings of why this should be the case. The main challenge remains *how*. There is an emerging consensus, however, about the kinds of professional development most likely to effect change.

Democracy is a recurring feature in successful CPD: teachers are allowed to take ownership of change as part of a 'community of practice' (CoP)(Lave & Wenger, 1991). In a CoP, people with a common interest collaborate over an extended period, sharing ideas and finding solutions to problems. The two case studies which follow both illustrate the power of collaboration of this kind and point to possible ways forward: the first reports the findings of the Secondary School Literacy Initiative Project (SSLI)(May & Smyth, 2007) in Aotearoa/New Zealand. The second also focuses on Aotearoa/New Zealand and the Te Kotāhitanga program (Bishop *et al.*, 2007) where teachers working with the Māori community have been attempting to improve educational outcomes for Māori students.

Case study: What teachers say they need

The Secondary Schools' Literacy Initiative (SSLI) involved a group of 60 pilot secondary schools in Aotearoa/New Zealand, 2003–2005. A regional facilitator was responsible for promoting and supporting a literacy focus within and across a cluster of schools. Within the schools, a literacy leader provided leadership and mentoring as part of ongoing professional support for colleagues. At the end of this process, Smyth (2007) reports how participating teachers were able to identify the following needs:

- Supportive and active spaces within which to learn about and act out, reaffirm or reframe their pedagogical approaches to literacy.
- Teaching contexts in which it is expected, and teachers are encouraged, to take risks and experiment with their teaching, in the knowledge that risk-taking is a normal part of being a literacy teacher.
- Circumstances in which they can get to know their students as human beings, which might mean working collaboratively with colleagues in jointly planning and evaluating literacy learning experiences for students. It can also involve sharing knowledge with colleagues about students' lives and the impact this has on their learning.
- Opportunities to develop collective understandings and pedagogical repertoires about what may 'make a difference' in literacy practices, especially with students who present with the most complex lives and the most complicated learning difficulties.
- Assistance in developing authentic forms of reporting student progress in literacy that are not simply about satisfying policy accountability requirements, but that are about creating genuine dialogical partnerships about student progress between students, teachers and parents.
- Shared understandings about how to most effectively create the learning conditions for student voice in which students' lives, experiences and aspirations are brought into conversation with valued literacy knowledge of the school and in which students have a measure of ownership of their learning.
- Collegiality and forms of solidarity with which to confront and contest ill-informed and ideologically driven agendas on what constitutes literacy in schools.
- Leadership support in establishing and maintaining the legitimacy of a literacy focus across the school and the curriculum.
- Creating a culture in which teachers are not afraid of data but rather regard them as an important resource with which to track and diagnose student literacy progress so as to inform their teaching practices and the learning of their students.

Case study: The Te Kotāhitanga program

Researchers involved in the Te Kotāhitanga program identified a serious mismatch between the opinions of teachers and the Māori community about the causes for the underachievement of Māori students. Most teachers adopted a deficit position: they located responsibility for underachievement in the home, low aspirations, lack of motivation and poor behavior. Parents and students, in contrast, saw relationships with teachers as the key issue. Most students expressed concerns about how teachers related to and interacted with them; parents, too, attached great importance to the quality of children's relationships with teachers.

Discussions with the Māori students, the Māori community and teachers led to the development of the Effective Teaching Profile which formed the basis for the Te Kotāhitanga program. Informed by the value system of the Māori community, the expectations were that teachers should:

- care for students as 'culturally located individuals';
- have high expectations;
- manage their classrooms in ways which promote learning, reducing reliance on transmission modes of education and using strategies that facilitate interactive learning;
- promote, monitor and reflect on learning outcomes and share this knowledge with the students.

The program gradually expanded from four pilot schools to 33 and focused on the teachers of Years 9 and 10 students. Ongoing observations of classroom practice, and interactive feedback sessions encouraged teachers to think critically about their teaching practice, and to introduce them to concepts and techniques supportive of Māori student learning. Co-construction meetings, where teachers jointly agreed on goals for improving learning outcomes, also played an important role: following the meetings, a facilitator worked with each of the teachers to achieve the goals.

Teachers responded enthusiastically about the level of support they received. Equally important, in CPD that focused on teachers' hearts and minds and, in many cases, challenged deeply entrenched negative attitudes, there was evidence of real learning:

> I mean you go through teachers' college and there, it is such a Pākehā [European] focus and there are Pākehā teachers teaching about Māori concepts. And this is the first time I actually felt like we had Māori people coming in and saying, 'This is what we would like you to do, this is how you can teach these kids. This is what will be effective.' So that worked for me and that was new.

The wider school community

When teaching is seen as a collective rather than an individual enterprise as in the Aotearoa/ New Zealand case studies, tacit knowledge is converted into explicit, shared ideas; in the process, teachers develop the capacity to self-reflect, to examine student performance and act on their own understandings. For change to be meaningful and sustainable, however, this 'collegiality' must extend beyond the school to the wider community (Fullan, 2007).

Te Kotāhitanga offers an example of the importance in reaching out in its consultations with Māori parents and students. Although there is a growing recognition of parents as essential partners, all too often they are excluded from their children's formal schooling. Sometimes this happens because teachers relate more easily to families who share their cultural norms and values. On other occasions, they fail to understand that there are other ways of 'doing literacy'. When children experience disjuncture between home and school they fail to thrive; when teachers cannot understand why children are underachieving the simplest course of action is to blame the victim, as indeed was the case in Te Kotāhitanga.

Parents position themselves in different ways to formal schooling. Some have internalized the traditional view that the main responsibility for literacy learning lies with teachers; others seek more active involvement. In all cases, however, we lose sight of one fundamental truth at our peril: parents care deeply about their children's education. This is demonstrated, for instance, by the hundreds of thousands of complementary schools set up by parents throughout the English-speaking world and Western Europe to teach their children to be literate in minority languages.

Attempts to involve parents are likely to succeed only when there is a willingness to accept parents on their own terms. Joint goals and activities need to be negotiated; they cannot simply be imposed.

Sub-Saharan Africa: a special case?

Any discussion of CPD in Africa needs to take account of the broader issues concerning education, the state and development (Christie *et al.*, 2005). There is, of course, great variation. In the Democratic Republic of Congo, the formal education system is currently in disarray and there is therefore no CPD. In more politically stable countries, it would appear that CPD is used primarily to orient teachers to new syllabuses or curricula which are determined by the priorities of foreign donors. Efforts to move teachers from the role of technician to reflective practitioner pose particular challenges for those wishing to encourage learner-centered pedagogies which may be seen as threatening teachers' authority (Tabulawa, 1997). Africa, then, may seem an unlikely place for the development of parent–teacher partnerships.

Based on Marriote Ngwaru's (2008) research in rural Zimbabwe, the case study that follows describes the birth of a home–school partnership. It shows that entrenched attitudes on the part of both parents and teachers can be successfully challenged even in the most adverse circumstances, laying the foundations for a growth view of CPD and the development of teachers as reflective practitioners.

Case study: School–home partnerships in Zimbabwe

Chitubu Primary School serves a rural community in Zimbabwe where parents and children live in the shadow of AIDS, poverty and political instability. Discussions with teachers at the start of the project suggested that parents played no part in the formal schooling of their children. Parents confirmed this was the case, explaining that that they were happy that the teachers knew what they were doing. Mr Ripei, for instance, offered: 'No, we do not know anything about what happens at school ... We help by forcing them to go to school because they do not know the importance of schooling'.

Comments such as this had suggested that attempts to establish a partnership between parents and teachers would be problematic. This was not the case. About 50 parents, all pupils and teachers attended a meeting instigated by a request from parents for the researcher to explain his preliminary findings. Contrary to expectations, parents demonstrated their readiness to become partners in literacy.

The meeting was opened by Mr Nyoka, a respected community elder with a prayer which framed literacy as the Holy Spirit filling the children through the agency of the head of the school and her assistants. Mr Gamba, another elder, used further epithets of salvation and blessings:

> As I stand here I am also one overflowing with joy. I am thrilled about the great event that has brought great happiness to our school. We have never seen anything like this and therefore, before I make my presentation, I would like to lead you into song ... This means we have just had a new-born baby just like Jesus here at our school. It is a pleasant miracle that has happened here ... Children have come with reports of this project home and the benefits it has brought.

This imagery underlines the value the community attached to the literacy. What comes through is the joy of parents in actively participating, in marked contrast to the views expressed in the interviews earlier that they had no role to play in school learning. This enthusiasm clearly has the potential to be transformed into participation in the day-to-day activities of the school.

Parents and children are essential partners in reform at school level. But, as Fullan (2007) points out, for change to be both meaningful and sustainable, 'collegiality' needs also to extend to other schools at local and national levels.

International collaboration

Collaboration on many different levels is one of the recurring themes of this book. By working together, whole school communities are able to take ownership of attempts to improve the educational outcomes for their students. In the case of SSLI and Te Kotāhitanga, this collaboration took place in the context of whole school improvement initiatives in the industrialized world; in the case of Chitubu Primary School, resources were far more limited. In Africa more generally, access to the *what, why* and *how* of training is extremely limited in both initial teacher education and in continuing professional development. Traditional pedagogies prevail in settings where the continued use of ex-colonial languages has the effect of disenfranchising the majority of the population.

Although conditions in industrialized and developing countries are very different, teachers in both settings have a shared interest in supporting linguistically diverse students. As you will recall, communities of practice involve people with a common interest collaborating over an extended period to find solutions to problems. There is no requirement, however, for physical proximity. In a world where electronic communication and international travel have become commonplace, there are also opportunities for *virtual* communities of practice. I will end then with a case study, based on Rassool *et al.* (2007), of a project which points to the potential of international collaboration in finding solutions to the problems of ensuring effective literacy teaching in multilingual settings.

Case study: Knowledge transfer: a UK–South African experience

Materials produced for a 1995–98 initiative in England on 'Meeting the needs of bilingual pupils in the mainstream classroom' were the starting point for collaboration between colleagues at the University of Reading, UK, and the Project for Alternative Education at the University of Cape Town, South Africa (PRAESA).

When any materials are transferred from one setting to another, they need to be adapted to suit local conditions. Many of the modifications required in this case were of a superficial nature: photographs required to illustrate an exercise on stereotyping, for instance, needed to reflect the population of South Africa rather than the UK. In other cases, elements were omitted: an activity designed to draw attention to the difficulties of learning a new script was not relevant in South Africa where all languages are written in a roman script.

It was important to acknowledge – and exploit – differences between South African and British teachers. Most UK teachers have little personal experience of bilingualism. Most teachers in Southern Africa, in contrast, are bilingual or even multilingual and are therefore better able to relate to the situation of children being educated through a language which is not their mother tongue. Building on this experience, an activity included in the South African pack invites participants to shade or color different parts of an outline drawing of a body to reflect the languages that they speak. As one teacher who undertook this exercise commented: 'Gold is Otijherero, my precious language, the language of my heart'.

UK expertise was valuable in production. The experience of having produced the original training packs was useful in determining both the different elements that would be necessary in the development of the South African materials and aspects of project management. As part of the same process, British participants were able to upgrade South African colleagues' skills in IT, presentation and design.

Acutely aware of historical power imbalances between the United Kingdom and South Africa, we were concerned that the project should not replicate the one-way model of knowledge transfer – from the metropolitan, ex-colonial 'mother-country' to the emerging post-colonial nation state. As we questioned our own assumptions and values, it became clear that we were in fact dealing with a two-way flow of knowledge and expertise. We had not envisaged, for instance, the extent to which the adaptation of the packs would help in the revision and improvement of the original materials.

The materials developed jointly by PRAESA and the University of Reading have been used extensively on courses offered to participants on courses from all over southern Africa. In particular, they have been a key component in the training of teachers in the implementation in the Western Cape Province of a bilingual education policy for the first six years of education. The materials have the potential to be used in a wide range of multilingual settings and can be downloaded free of charge from www.tell.praesa.org.

Key points

Teachers working in multilingual communities often find themselves reinventing pedagogical practices devised with monolingual, more culturally homogenous populations in mind. We have a much clearer idea today of *what* needs to be included in training and *why*. However, much work remains to be done on establishing *how* teachers can best be supported to make the necessary changes.

Traditional approaches to professional development have been criticized for a number of reasons: teachers are 'force fed' with information; more attention is paid to content than to learning processes; few attempt are made to meet the needs of teachers with differing levels of experience; and initiatives are piecemeal with little follow-up.

Effective professional development, in contrast, is:

- driven by a clear idea of the goals to be achieved;

- systemic: one-off workshops do not work because they fail to offer ongoing support for those charged with change or to involve all relevant members of the school community;

- an ongoing process: it is simply not enough to devote a few days a year to the current priority.

'Communities of practice' (CoP), where people with a common interest collaborate over an extended period, sharing ideas and finding solutions to problems, offer a promising way forward by offering teachers ownership of change. These CoP can be local or virtual.

Activities and discussion points

1. Think of a situation where you wanted to make a change to some aspect of your work or study. Were you successful? If so, think about the factors that contributed to your success. If not, identify the obstacles which stood in your way.

2. If you are a teacher, what CPD initiatives is your school involved in?
    (a)   Are the goals long term or short term?
    (b)   Do they encourage relective practice?
    (b)   Is there any planned follow-up?

Further reading

School improvement

Gray, J., Hopkins, D., Reynolds, D., Wilcox, B., Farrell, S. & Jesson, D. (1999) *Improving Schools: Performance and Potential*. Buckingham: Open University Press.

Teddlie, C. & Reynolds, D. (2000) *The International Handbook of School Effectiveness Research*. London: Falmer Press.

Fullan, M. (2007) *The New Meaning of Educational Change*. New York: Teachers College Press.

Professional development

Edwards, V., Rassool, N. & Bloch, C. (2007) Language and Development in Multilingual Settings: A Case Study of Knowledge Exchange and Teacher Education in South Africa. *International Review of Education* 52 (6): 533–52.

Guskey, T. (2000) *Evaluating Professional Development*. Thousand Oaks, CA: Corwin Press.

May, S. & Smyth, J. (eds) (2007) *Addressing Literacy in Secondary Schools*. Special issue of *Language and Education* 21 (5).

Key to Activity 1, p.81

Translation of Ik lees graag

I like reading

My name is Irene and I like reading.
I like reading long books
I like reading short books
I like reading funny books
I like reading sad books
I like reading books with pictures
I really like reading

You will have used some or all of the following features in making sense of this text

- The illustrations

- The repetition of key words and structures

- The use of cognates – or words with a common origin, e.g. *lang* is like *long*, and *boeke* is like *book* in English; *korte* is like *court* in French and *corto* in Spanish.

In looking at the sentence *Ik lees graag*, which word did you think meant *reading*? Most English speakers choose *graag*, based on English word order. Those who know German usually choose *lees* because of the similarity with *lezen* and this is, in fact, the correct answer.

If you made an incorrect choice, this is of little consequence. You were in fact behaving like an intelligent language learner making decisions on the basis of available information. With further exposure to Dutch you would find examples of both *lees* and *graag* which would lead you to modify your initial hypothesis.

References

Abu-Saad, I. (2007) The Portrayal of Arabs in Textbooks in the Jewish School System in Israel. *Arab Studies Quarterly*. Retrieved from: www.encyclopedia.com/doc/1G1-162883566.html.

ADEA/GTZ/Commonwealth Secretariat/UIE (2005) Optimizing Learning and Education in Africa – the Language Factor. A Stock-Taking Research on Mother Tongue and Bilingual Education in Sub-Saharan Africa. Retrieved from: www.adeanet.org/biennial2006/doc/document/B3_1_MTBLE_en.pdf.

Alexander, N. (ed.) (2005) *The Intellectualization of African languages: The African Academy of Languages and the Implementation of the Language Plan of Action for Africa*. Cape Town: PRAESA.

Allen, M. (2004) Reading Achievement of Students in French Immersion Programs. *Educational Quarterly Review* 9 (4): 25–30.

Allington, R. (2002) *Big Brother and the National Reading Curriculum: How Ideology Trumped Evidence*. Portsmouth, NH: Heinemann.

Anon. (2004) *Fun with Dick and Jane*. New York: Grosset & Dunlap.

An Ran (2000) Learning to read and write at home: the experience of Chinese families in Britain. In M. Martin-Jones & K. Jones (eds) *Multilingual Literacies: Reading and Writing in Different Worlds*. Amsterdam: John Benjamins, pp. 71–90.

An Ran (2001) Travelling on parallel tracks: Chinese parents and English teachers. *Educational Research* 43 (3): 311–28.

Apple, M. (1988) *Teachers and Texts: A Political Economy of Class and Gender Relations in Education*. London: Routledge.

Auerbach, E. (1992) Literacy and Ideology. *Annual Review of Applied Linguistics* 12: 71–85.

Australia (1991) *Australia's Language: The Australian Language and Literacy Policy*. Canberra: DEET.

Australia (2005) *Teaching Reading: A Review of the Evidence-Based Research Literature on Approaches to the Teaching of Literacy, Particularly Those That Are Effective in Assisting Students with Reading Difficulties*. Canberra: Department of Education, Science and Training.

Baker, C. (2003) Biliteracy and Transliteracy in Wales: Language Planning and the Welsh National Curriculum. In N. Hornberger (ed.) *Continua of Biliteracy: An Ecological Framework for Educational Policy, Research and Practice in Multilingual Settings*. Clevedon: Multilingual Matters, pp. 71–90.

Baker, C. (2006) *Foundations of Bilingual Education and Bilingualism*. Clevedon: Multilingual Matters.

Baker, C. & Hornberger, N. (eds) (2001) *An Introductory Reader to the Writings of Jim Cummins*. Clevedon: Multilingual Matters.

Baker, P. & Eversley, J. (eds) (2000) *Multilingual Capital: The Languages of London Schoolchildren and Their Relevance to Economic, Social and Educational Policies*. London: Battlebridge.

Baker, C. & Prys Jones, S. (1998) *Encyclopedia of Bilingualism and Bilingual Education*. Clevedon: Multilingual Matters.

Barron-Hauwaert, S. (2004) *Language Strategies for Bilingual Families: The One-Parent-One-Language Approach*. Clevedon: Multilingual Matters.

Basree Bt Abdul Rahman, S. (2007) The implementation of the Contemporary Children's Literature Program in Malaysian Primary Schools. Unpublished PhD thesis: University of Reading.

Baugh, A. & Cable, T. (2001) *A History of the English Language* (5th edn). Upper Saddle River, NJ: Prentice Hall.

Bishop, R., Berruman, M., Canvanagh, T. & Teddy, L. (2007) Te *Kōtahitanga Phase 3: Establishing a Culturally Responsive Pedagogy of Relations in Mainstream Secondary School Classrooms*. Auckland: Ministry of Education. Retrieved from: www.educationcounts.govt.nz/publications/series/te_kotahitanga/9454.

Blackledge, A. (1999) Language, Literacy and Social Justice: The Experiences of Bangladeshi Women in Birmingham, UK. *Journal of Multilingual and Multicultural Development* 20 (3): 179–93.

Blackledge, A. (2001) Complex Positionings: Women Negotiating Identity and Power in a Minority Urban Setting. In A. Pavlenko, A. Blackledge, I. Piller & M. Teutsch-Dwyer (eds) *Multilingualism, Second Language Learning, and Gender*. Berlin: Mouton de Gruyter, pp. 53–75.

Blackledge, A. (2004) *Negotiation of Identities in Multilingual Contexts*. Clevedon: Multilingual Matters.

Bloch, C. (2005) *Building Bridges between Oral and Written Language: Facilitating Reading Opportunities for Children in Africa*. Cape Town: PRAESA.

Bloch, C. (2007) *Theory and Strategy of Early Literacy in Contemporary Africa, with Special Reference to South Africa*. Cape Town: PRAESA Occasional Papers.

Bourdieu, P. (1991) *Language and Symbolic Power*. Cambridge, MA: Harvard University Press.

Bourdieu, P. (1997) The Forms of Capital. In A.H. Halsey, H. Lauder, P. Brown & A.S. Wells (eds) *Education, Culture, Economy, and Society*. Oxford: Oxford University Press, pp. 46–58.

Bowe, F. (1991) *Approaching Equality*. Silver Spring, MD: TJ Publishers.

Brooker, L. (2002) 'Five on the First of December!': What Can We Learn from Case Studies of Early Childhood Literacy? *Journal of Early Childhood Literacy* 2 (3): 291–313.

Bullock, S.A. (1975) *A Language for Life*. London: HMSO.

Busch, B. & Schick, J. (2006) Educational Materials Reflecting Heteroglossia: Disinventing Ethnolinguistic Differences in Bosnia-Herzegovina. In A. Pennycook & S. Makoni (eds) *Disinventing and Reinventing Language*. Clevedon: Multilingual Matters, pp. 216–32.

Camilli, G., Vargas, S. & Yurecko, M. (2003) 'Teaching Children to Read': The Fragile Link between Science and Federal Education Policy. *Education Policy Analysis Archives* 11 (15). Retrieved from: http://epaa.asu.edu/epaa/v11n5/.

Caravolas, M. (2005) The Nature and Causes of Dyslexia in Different Languages. In M. Snowling (ed.) *The Science of Reading: A Handbook*. Malden, MA: Blackwell, pp. 336–55.

Census of India (2001) *Note*. Retrieved From: www.Censusindia.Gov.In/Census_Data_2001/Census_Data_Online/Language/Gen_Note.htm

Chao, T.H. (1997) *Chinese Heritage Community Language Schools in the United States*. Retrieved from: www.cal.org/resources/digest/cha00001.html.

Chew, J. (2005) Editorial. *Reading Reform Foundation Newsletter* 55 (1).

Chick, J.K. (1996) Safetalk: Collusion in Apartheid Eucation. In H. Coleman (ed.) *Society and the Language Classroom*. Cambridge: Cambridge University Press, pp. 21–39.

Christie, P., Harley, K. & Penny, A. (2005) Case studies from Sub-Saaharan Africa. In C. Day & J. Sachs (eds) *International Handbook of Continuing Professional Development*. Buckingham: Open University Press, pp. 167–90.

CILT, National Centre for Language Teaching (2005) *Language Trends 2005: Community Language Learning in England, Wales and Scotland*. London: CILT. Retrieved from: www.cilt.org.uk/research/languagetrends/2005/trends2005_community.pdf.

Clark, C. & Rumbold, K. (2006) *Reading for Pleasure: A Research Overview*. London: National Literacy Trust. Retrieved from: www.literacytrust.org.uk/Research/readpleasure.html.

Coles, G. (2003) *Reading the Naked Truth: Literacy, Legislation, and Lies*. Portsmouth, NH: Heinemann.

Conrad, R. (1979) *The Deaf School Child*. London: Harper & Row.

Cook, V. & Bassetti, B. (eds) (2005) *Second Language Writing Systems*. Clevedon: Multilingual Matters.

Crawford, J. (1999) *Bilingual Education: History, Politics, Theory and Practice*. (4th edn). Los Angeles, CA: Bilingual Education Services.

Crawford, J. (2005) *No Child Left Behind: Misguided Approach to School Accountability for English Language Learners*. *NABE News* January/February Retrieved from: www.nabe.org/documents/policy_legislation/NABE_on_NCLB.pdf.

Crawford, J. (2008) *Advocating for English Learners*. Clevedon: Multilingual Matters.

Crystal, D. (2003) *English as a Global Language*. Cambridge: Cambridge University Press.

Cummins, J. (2001) *Negotiating Identities: Education for Empowerment in a Diverse Society*. Ontario, CA: California Association for Bilingual Education.

Cummins, J., Bismilla, V., Chow, P., Cohen, S., Giampapa, F., Leoni, L., Sandhu, P. & Sastri, P. (2005) Affirming Identity in Multilingual Classrooms. *Educational Leadership* 63 (1): 38–43.

Davies, F.W.J. (1973) *Teaching Reading in Early England*. London: Pitman and Sons Ltd.

Davison, C. (2001) Identity and Ideology: The Problem of Defining and Defending ESL-ness. In B. Mohan, C. Leung & C. Davison (eds) *English as a Second Language in the Mainstream: Teaching Learning and Identity*. Harlow: Longman Pearson, pp. 71–90.

De Castell, S., Luke, A. & Luke, C. (eds) (1989) *Language, Authority and Criticism: Readings on the School Textbook*. London: Falmer Press.

Del Valle, S. (2003) *Language Rights and the Law in the United States: Finding our Voices*. Clevedon: Multilingual Matters.

Denton, C., Anthony, J., Parker, R. & Hasbrouck, J. (2004) Effects of Two Tutoring Programs on the English Reading Development of Spanish–English. *Bilingual Students Elementary School Journal* 104: 289–305.

DfEE (Department for Education and Employment) (1998) *Homework: Guidelines for Primary and Secondary Schools*. London: DfEE.

Du Plessis, L. (2003) Multilingualism in Public Institutions like Libraries. Retrieved from: www.fs.gov. za/Departments/SAC/Library/multilingualism_jul-sept2003_main_article_main.htm.

Education and Science Committee (2001) *Me Panui Tatou Katoa – Let's All Read: Report of the Education and Science Committee on the Inquiry into the Teaching of Reading in New Zealand.* Wellington, New Zealand: House of Representatives.

Edwards, V. (1995) *Reading in Multilingual Classrooms.* Reading: Reading and Language Information Centre.

Edwards, V. (2004) *Multilingualism in the English-Speaking World: Pedigree of Nations.* Oxford: Blackwell.

Edwards, V. (2007a) Language, Diversity and Education in Europe: Implications for Resources. In A. Papapavlou & P. Pavlou (eds) *Sociolinguistic and Pedagogical Dimensions of Dialects in Education.* Newcastle: Cambridge Scholars Publishing, pp. 34–49.

Edwards, V. (2007b) The economics of minority languages: Promotion and publishing. Paper presented at the 11th International Conference on Minority Languages, Pecs, Hungary, 5–7 July.

Edwards, V. (2008a) *The Culture of Reading: An Evaluation of a Key Programme of PRAESA.* Cape Town: PRAESA.

Edwards, V. (2008b) The New Minority Languages in the UK. In G. Extra & D. Gorter (eds) *The European Constellation of Languages: Facts and Policies.* Berlin: Mouton de Gruyter.

Edwards, V. & Pritchard Newcombe, L. (2005) When School Is Not Enough. *International Journal of Bilingualism and Bilingual Education* 8 (4): 298–312.

Edwards, V. & Rassool, N. (2007) A Review of the Literature on Approaches to the Use of Phonics, Including Synthetic Phonics, in the Teaching of Reading in Primary Schools and Early Years Settings. Appendix to *Improving the Learning and Teaching of Early Reading Skills.* Cardiff: Estyn, Her Majesty's Inspectorate for Education and Training in Wales. Retrieved from: www.estyn.gov.uk/publications/Improving_the_Learning_and_Teaching_of_Early_Reading_Skills_June_2007.pdf.

Edwards, V., Monaghan, F. & Knight, J. (2000) Books, Pictures and Conversations: Using Bilingual Multimedia Storybooks to Develop Language Awareness. *Language Awareness* 9: 135–16

Edwards, V., Pemberton, L., Knight, J. & Monaghan, F. (2002) Fabula: A Multimedia Authoring Environment for Children Exploring Minority Languages. *Language Learning and Technology* 6 (2): 59–69.

Ellis, L. A. (2005) *Balancing Approaches: Revisiting the Educational Psychology Research on Teaching Students with Learning Difficulties.* Camberwell, Victoria: Australian Council for Educational Research.

Europa (2006) Commission ready to welcome three new official languages on 1 January 2007. Retrieved from: http://europa.eu/rapid/pressReleasesAction.do?reference=IP/06/1854&format=HTML&aged=0&language=EN&guiLanguage=en.

Extra, G. & Gorter, D. (eds) (2001) *The Other Languages of Europe.* Clevedon: Multilingual Matters.

Feuverger, G. (1994) A Multicultural Literacy Intervention for Minority Language Students. *Language and Education* 8 (3): 123–46.

Feynman, R. & Leighton, R. (1997) *Surely You're Joking, Mr. Feynman!: Adventures of a Curious Character.* New York: W.W. Norton.

Fishman, J. (1991) *Reversing Language Shift: Theoretical and Empirical Foundations of Assistance to Threatened Languages*. Clevedon: Multilingual Matters.

Fishman, J. (2001) *Can Threatened Languages Be Saved: Reversing Language Shift, Revisited: A 21st Century Perspective*. Clevedon: Multilingual Matters.

Francis, N. and Reyhner, J. (eds) (2002) *Language and Literacy Teaching for Indigenous Education: A Bilingual Approach*. Clevedon: Multilingual Matters.

Freebody, P. (2001) Theorising New Literacies In and Out of School. *Language and Education* 15 (2&3): 105–16.

Freire, P. (1970) *Pedagogy of the Oppressed*. London: Continuum.

Fullan, M. (2007) *The New Meaning of Educational Change*. New York: Teachers College Press.

García, O. (2008) *Bilingual Education in the 21st Century: A Global Perspective*. Oxford: Blackwell.

Gee, J.P. (1991) Socio-Cultural Approaches to Literacy. *Annual Review of Applied Linguistics* 12: 31–48.

Giroux, H. (1992) *Border Crossings: Cultural Workers and the Politics of Education*. London: Routledge.

González, N., Moll, L. & Amanti, C. (eds) (2005) *Funds of Knowledge: Theorizing Practices in Households and Classrooms*. Mahwah, NJ: Lawrence Erlbaum.

Goodman, K.S. (1967) Reading: A Psycholinguistic Guessing Game. *Journal of the Reading Specialist* 6 (4): 126–35.

Goodman, K.S. (2005) *What's Whole in Whole Language: 20th Anniversary Edition*. Muskegon, MI: RDR Books.

Graddol, D. (2006) *English Next*. London: The British Council. Retrieved from: www.britishcouncil. org/learning-research-englishnext.htm.

Graff, H. (1991) *The Literacy Myth: Cultural Integration and Social Structure in the Nineteenth*. New York: Academic Press.

Grant, M. (2005) *Accelerated Reading and Writing with Synthetic Phonics and Virtual Elimination of the 'Tail of Underachievement': A Seven Year Longitudinal Study*. Retrieved from: www. ridgehillpublishing.com/images/RPadd_ins/Accerlerated%20reading%20and%20writing.pdf.

Gray, J., Hopkins, D., Reynolds, D., Wilcox, B., Farrell, S. & Jesson, D. (1999) *Improving Schools: Performance and Potential*. Buckingham: Open University Press.

Gregory, E. (1993) Sweet and Sour: Learning to Read in a British and a Chinese School. *English in Education* 27 (3): 53–9.

Gregory, E. (1996) Learning from the Community: A Family Literacy Project with Bangladeshi-Origin Children in London. In S. Wolfendale & K. Topping (eds) *Family Involvement in Literacy. Effective Partnerships in Education*. London: Cassell, pp. 89–102.

Gregory, E. (1998) Siblings as Mediators of Literacy in Linguistic Minority Communities. *Language and Education* 12 (1): 33–54.

Grierson, G.A. (1928) *Linguistic Survey of India Vol I–XI*. Calcutta. Reprinted Delhi: Motilal Banarsidas, 1967–1968.

Gurnah, A. (2001) Languages and Literacies for Autonomy. In M. Martin-Jones & K. Jones (eds) *Multilingual Literacies: Reading and Writing in Different Worlds*. Amsterdam: John Benjamins, pp. 233–45.

Guskey, T. (2000) *Evaluating Professional Development*. Thousand Oaks, CA: Corwin Press.

Häggsblom, C. (2006) *Young EFL Pupils Reading Multicultural Fiction: An Ethnographic Case Study of a Swedish Language Primary School in Finland*. Turku: Åbo Akademi.

Haldeman, S. (2007) *Pennsylvania Dutch: A Dialect Of South German With An Infusion Of English*. Whitefish, MT: Kessinger Publishing.

Hall, N. (2003). The Child in the Middle: Agency and Diplomacy in Language Brokering Events. In G. Hansen, K. Malmkjaer & D. Gile (eds) *Claims, Changes and Challenges in Translation Studies*. Amsterdam: John Benjamins.

Harlow, B. & Carter, M. (2003) *Archives of Empire volume 11: the Scramble for Africa*. Raleigh, NC: Duke University Press.

Hayes, D. (2000) Cascade Training and Teachers' Professional Development. *ELT Journal* 54 (2): 135–45.

Heath, S.B. (1983) *Ways with Words: Language, Life and Work in Communities and Classrooms*. Cambridge: Cambridge University Press.

Henevald, W. & Craig, H. (1996) *Schools Count: World Bank Project Designs and the Quality of Primary Education in Sub-Saharan Africa*. Washington, DC: World Bank.

Hirsch, Jr, E.D. (1987) *Cultural Literacy: What Every American Needs to Know*. Boston: Houghton Mifflin.

Hoerder, D. (2002) *Cultures in Contact: World Migrations in the Second Millennium*. Durham, NC: Duke University Press.

Holm, J. (2000) *An Introduction to Pidgins and Creoles*. Cambridge: Cambridge University Press.

Hornberger, N. (2000) Afterword: Multilingual Literacies, Literacy Practices and the Continua of Biliteracy. In M. Martin-Jones & K. Jones (eds) *Multilingual Literacies: Reading and Writing Different Worlds*. Amsterdam: John Benjamins, pp. 353–67.

Hornberger, N. & Skilton-Sylvester, E. (2003) Revisiting the Continua of Biliteracy: International and Critical Perspectives. In E. Skilton-Sylvester (ed.) *Continua of Biliteracy: An Ecological Framework for Educational Policy, Research and Practice in Multilingual Settings*. Clevedon: Multilingual Matters, pp. 35–67.

Hornberger, N. (ed.) (2003) *Continua of Biliteracy: An Ecological Framework for Educational Policy, Research and Practice in Multilingual Settings*. Clevedon: Multilingual Matters.

Howard, E. & Sugarman, J. (2007) *Realizing the Vision of Two-Way Immersion: Fostering Effective Programs and Classrooms*. Malden, MA: Delta Publishing.

HREOC (Human Rights and Equal Opportunities Commission) (1992) *Bringing Them Home: Report of the National Inquiry into the Separation of Aboriginal and Torres Strait Islander Children from Their Families*. Sydney: HREOC.

Hudelson, S. (1989) *Write On: Children Writing in ESL*. Old Tappan, NJ: Prentice Hall Regents.

Hutchinson, J., Whiteley, H., Smith, C. & Connors, L. (2003) The Developmental Progression of Comprehension-Related Skills in Children Learning EAL. *Journal of Research in Reading* 26: 19–32.

Japan Times (2007) Okinawa Slams History Text Rewrite. *Japan Times Online* 23 June. Retrieved from: http://search.japantimes.co.jp/cgi-bin/nn20070623a1.html.

Jenkins, G. (1993) *The Foundations of Modern Wales 1642–1780*. Oxford: Oxford University Press.

Jessner, U. (2006) *Linguistic Awareness in Multilinguals*. Edinburgh: Edinburgh University Press.

Johnston, R.S. & Watson, J.E. (2005) *The Effects of Synthetic Phonics Teaching on Reading and Spelling Attainment: A Seven-Year Longitudinal Study*. Edinburgh: Scottish Education Executive.

Kagan, O., Bauckus, S. & Brinton, D. (eds) (2007) *Heritage Language Education: A New Field Emerging*. Mahwah, NJ: Lawrence Erlbaum.

Kamwangamalu, N. (2000) A New Language Policy, Old Language Practices: Status Planning for African Languages in a Multilingual South Africa. *South African Journal of African Languages* 20 (1): 50–60.

Kapur, M. (1997) *Babu's Day*. Panjabi translation by SS Attariwala. London: Mantra.

Kelly, C., Gregory, E. & Williams, A. (2001) Home to School and School to Home: Syncretised Literacies in Linguistic Minority Communities. *Language, Culture and Curriculum* 14 (1): 9–25.

Kenner, C. (2004) *Becoming Biliterate: Young Children Learning Different Writing Systems*. Stoke-on-Trent: Trentham Books.

Kenner, C., Gregory, E., Jessel, J., Ruby, M. & Arju, T. (2007) Intergenerational Learning between Children and Grandparents in East London. *Journal of Early Childhood Research* 5: 219–43.

Kerswill, P. (2006) Migration and Language. In K. Mattheier, U. Ammon & P. Trudgill (eds) *Sociolinguistics. An International Handbook of the Science of Language and Society*, 2nd edn, Vol 2. Berlin: De Gruyter. Retrieved from: www.ling.lancs.ac.uk/staff/kerswill/pkpubs.htm.

Kinealy, C. (1995) *This Great Calamity: The Irish Famine 1845–52*. Basingstoke: Gill & Macmillan.

Knapp, K. & Meierkord, C. (eds) (2002) *Lingua Franca Communication*. Frankfurt am Main: Peter Lang.

Kouwenberg, S. (2007) *Handbook of Pidgins and Creoles*. Oxford and Malden, MA: Blackwell.

Labov, W. (1982) Objectivity and Commitment in Linguistic Science: The Case of the Black English Trial in Ann Arbor. *Language in Society* 11 (2): 165–202.

Ladd, P. (2003) *Understanding Deaf Culture: In Search of Deafhood*. Clevedon: Multilingual Matters.

Lave, J. & Wenger, E. (1991) *Situated Learning: Legitimate Peripheral Participation*. Cambridge: Cambridge University Press.

Lechner, F. & Boli, J. (eds) (2004) *The Globalization Reader*. Malden, MA: Wiley-Blackwell.

Lewis, G. (2007) *Letter to CS Lewis*. Commissioned by BBC Radio 4's Today programme, 31 December.

Lindholm-Leary, K. (2000) *Biliteracy for a Global Society: An Idea Book on Dual Language Education*. Washington, DC: George Washington University. Retrieved from: www.ncela.gwu.edu/resabout/programs/5_native.html.

Luke, A. (1988) *Literacy, Textbooks, and Ideology*. London: Falmer Press.

Macedo, D. & Freire, P. (1987) *Literacy: Reading the Word and the World*. Westport, CT: Bergin & Garvey.

Mallikarjun, B. (2001) Language According to Census 2001. *Language in India* 1 (2): Retrieved from: www.languageinindia.com/april2001/indiancensus.html.

Manning, P. (2005) *Migration in World History*. London: Routledge.

Masny, D. & Ghahremani-Ghajar, S. (1999) Weaving Multiple Literacies: Somali Children and Their Teachers in the Context of School Culture. *Language, Culture and Curriculum* 12 (1): 72–93.

May, S. (2001) *Language and Minority Rights: Ethnicity, Nationalism and the Politics of Language*.London: Longman.

May, S. & Smyth, J. (eds) (2007) Addressing Literacy in Secondary Schools. Special issue of *Language and Education* 21 (5): 365–9.

May, S., Hill, R. & Tiakiwai, S. (2006) *Bilingual/Immersion Education: Indicators of Good Practice*. Wellington: Ministry of Education.

McKeown, A. (2004) Global Migration 1846–1940. *Journal of World History* 15 (2): 155–89.

McKinney, C. (2005) *Textbooks for Diverse Learners: A Critical Analysis of Learning Materials Used in South African Schools*. Cape Town: HSRC Press.

McQuillan, J. & Tse, L. (1996) Does Research Really Matter? An Analysis of Media Opinion on Bilingual Education, 1984–1994. *Bilingual Research Journal* 20 (1): 1–27.

McWilliam, N. (1998) *What's in a Word? Vocabulary Development in Multilingual Classrooms*. Stoke-on-Trent: Trentham.

Mercator Education (undated) *The Basque Language in Education*. Retrieved from: www1.fa.knaw.nl/mercator/regionale_dossiers/regional_dossier_basque_in_spain2nd.htm.

Michael, A. (1989) Textbook Publishing: The Political and Economic Influences. *Theory into Practice* 28 (4): 282–87.

Multilingual Resources for Children Project (MRC) (1995) *Building Bridges: Multilingual Resources for Children*. Clevedon: Multilingual Matters.

Myers-Scotton, C. 1993. Elite closure as a powerful language strategy: the African case. *International Journal of Sociology of Language* 103: 149–63.

Nadeau, J.B. & Barlow, J. (2008) *The Story of French*. New York: St. Martin's Griffin.

Nardo, D. (2006) *The Age of Colonialism*. Chicago: Lucent Books.

National Reading Panel (NRP) (2000) *Teaching Children to Read: An Evidence-Based Assessment of the Scientific Research Literature on Reading and Its Implications for Reading Instruction. Reports of the Subgroups*. Bethesda, MD: National Reading Panel.

New London Group (1996) A Pedagogy of Multiliteracies Designing Social Futures. *Harvard Educational Review* 66 (1). Retrieved from: wwwstatic.kern.org/filer/blogWrite44ManilaWebsite/paul/articles/A_Pedagogy_of_Multiliteracies_Designing_Social_Futures.htm.

Ngwaru, M. (2008) Literacy and Learning at Home and in School in a Rural Zimbabwean Community. Unpublished PhD thesis: University of Reading.

Norton, B. (2000) *Identity and Language Learning: Gender, Ethnicity and Educational Change*. Harlow: Pearson Education.

OECD (Organisation for Economic Cooperation and Development) (2002) *Reading for Change: Performance and Engagement across Countries. Results from Pisa 2000*. New York: OECD.

Opoku-Amankwa, K. (2008) Textbooks, Classroom Communication and Literacy Development in a Multilingual School in Ghana. Unpublished PhD thesis: University of Reading.

Pahl, K. & Rowsell, J. (eds) (2006) *Travel Notes from the New Literacy Studies*. Clevedon: Multilingual Matters.

Paterson, F. (2000) The Politics of Phonics. *Journal of Curriculum and Supervision* 15: 179–211.

Pearson, P. (2004) The Reading Wars. *Educational Policy* 18 (1): 216–52.

Pennycook, A. (1994) *The Cultural Politics of English as an International Language*. Harlow: Longman.

Pennycook, A. & Makoni, S. (eds) (2007) *Disinventing and Reinventing Language*. Clevedon: Multilingual Matters.

Perry, T. & Delpit, L. (eds) (1997) *The Real Ebonics Debate: Power, Language, and the Education of African–American Children*. Special issue of *Rethinking Schools*. Retrieved from: www.rethinkingschools.org/publication/ebonics/ebotoc.shtml.

Phillipson, R. (2000) *Linguistic Imperialism*. Oxford: Oxford University Press.

Prez, B. (2003) *Becoming Biliterate: A Study of Two-Way Bilingual Immersion Education*. Mahwah, NJ: Lawrence Erlbaum

Purdie, N. & Ellis, N. (2005) *A Review of the Empirical Evidence Identifying Effective Interventions and Teaching Practices for Students with Learning Difficulties in Years 4, 5 and 6*. Camberwell, Victoria: Australian Council for Educational Research.

Ramírez, D., Wiley, T., De Klerk, G., Lee, E. & Wright, W. (2005) *Ebonics: The Urban Education Debate* (2nd edn). Clevedon: Multilingual Matters.

Ramírez, J., Yuen, S. & Ramey, E. (1991) *Final Report: Longitudinal Study of Structured English Immersion Strategy, Early Exit and Late-Exit Transitional Bilingual Education Programs for Language Minority Children*. US Department of Education Contract No. 300-87-0156. Sguirre International, San Mateo, CA.

Rassool, N., Canvin, M., Heugh, K. & Mansoor, S. (2007) *Global Issues in Language, Education and Development*. Clevedon: Multilingual Matters.

Reader, D. (1989) *A Lovely Bunch of Coconuts*. London: Walker Books.

Robertson, L. H. (2006) Learning to Read 'Properly' by Moving between Parallel Literacy Classes. *Language and Education* 20 (1): 44–61.

Rose, J. (2006) *Independent Review of the Teaching of Early Reading*. London: Department of Children, Schools and Families. Retrieved from: www.standards.dcsf.gov.uk/eyfs/resources/downloads/report.pdf.

Rosenberg, D. (ed.) (2000) *Books for Schools: Improving Access to Supplementary Reading Materials in Africa*. Paris: ADEA.

Rosowsky, A. (2001) Decoding as a Cultural Practice and Its Effects on the Reading Process of Bilingual Pupils. *Language and Education* 15 (1): 56–70.

Rosowsky, A. (2008) *Heavenly Readings: Liturgical Literacy in a Multilingual Context.* Clevdeon: Multilingual Matters.

Seymour, P. (2005) Early Reading Development in European Orthographies. In M. Snowling (ed.) *The Science of Reading: A Handbook.* Malden, MA: Blackwell, pp. 296–315.

Sharifian, F., Rochecouste, J., Malcolm I.G., Konigsberg, P. & Collard, G. (2004) *Improving Understanding of Aboriginal Literacy: Factors in Text Comprehension. A Project of the ABC of Two-Way Literacy and Learning.* East Perth: Department of Education and Training.

Skutnabb-Kangas, T. (2000) *Linguistic Genocide in Education – or Worldwide Diversity and Human Rights?* Mahwah, NJ: Lawrence Erlbaum.

Smitherman, G. (1997) *Talkin and Testifyin: The Language of Black America.* Detroit, MI: Wayne State University Press.

Smyth, J. (2007) Pedagogy, School Culture and Teacher Learning: Towards More Durable and Resistant Approaches to Secondary School Literacy. *Language and Education* 21 (5): 406–19.

Sneddon, R. (2008) Magda and Albana – Learning to Read with Dual Language Books. *Language and Education* 22 (2): 137–54.

Soler, J. (2001) *Managerialist Discourse, the Literacy Standards Debate, and the Shaping of the English National Literacy Strategy.* Paper presented at the Conference of the Australian Association for Research in Education (AARE), University of Queensland.

Solity, J. (2003) *Teaching Phonics in Context: A Critique of the National Literacy Strategy Contents.* London: Department for Education and Science. Retrieved from: www.standards.dfes.gov.uk/ primary/ publications/literacy/686807/nls_phonics0303jsolity.pdf.

Statistics Canada (1998) Canada's Aboriginal Languages. Retrieved from: www.statcan.ca/Daily/ English/981214/d981214.htm.

Stearns, P. (2004) *The Industrial Revolution in World History.* Boulder, CO: Westview Press.

Stokes, P. (2000) *The Somali Community in Liverpool: A Report for a Commission of Enquiry.* Birmingham: Foundation for Civil Society.

Street, B. (1984) *Literacy in Theory and Practice.* Cambridge: Cambridge University Press.

Street, B. (ed.) (1997) Social Literacies. In V. Edwards & D. Corson (eds) *Encyclopedia of Language and Education,* Vol 2: *Literacy.* Dordrecht: Kluwer, pp. 133–41.

Stuart, M. (2004) Getting Ready for Reading: A Follow-up Study of Inner City Second Language Learners at the End of Key Stage 1. *British Journal of Educational Psychology* 74: 15–36.

Stuart, J. & Kunje, D. (2000) The Malawi Integrated In-Service Teacher Education Project: An Analysis of the Curriculum and Its Delivery in the Colleges. Centre for International Education, University of Sussex. Retrieved from: www.sussex.ac.uk/education/1-4-30-8-8.html.

Swann, L. (1985) *Education for All.* London: HMSO.

Swanwick, R. & Gregory, S. (2007) *Sign Bilingual Education: Policy and Practice.* Coleford, Gloucestershire: Forest Books.

Tabulawa, R. (1997) Pedagogical Classroom Practice and the Social Context: The Case of Botswana. *International Journal of Education Development*. 14 (1): 65–73.

Taylor, B., Pearson, P., Peterson, D. & Rodriguez, M. (2005) The Ciera School Change Framework: An Evidenced-Based Approach to Professional Development and School Reading Improvement. *Reading Research Quarterly* 40 (1): 40–69.

Teddlie, C. & Reynolds, D. (2000) *The International Handbook of School Effectiveness Research*. London: Falmer Press.

Thomas, W. & Collier, V. (2002) *Summary of Findings across All Research Sites. A National Study of School Effectiveness for Language Minority Students' Long-Term Achievement*. Final Report: Project 1.1. Santa Cruz, CA: Center for Research on Education, Diversity and Excellence, University of California.

Thornton, R. (1987) *American Indian Holocaust and Survival: A Population History Since 1492*. Norman, OK: University of Oklahoma Press.

Topping, K. (1992) Short and Long Term Follow-up of Parental Involvement in Reading Projects. *British Educational Research Journal* 18 (4): 369–79.

Torgerson, C., Brooks, G. & Hall, J. (2006) *A Systematic Review of the Research Literature on the Use of Phonics in the Teaching of Reading and Spelling*. Research Report Rr711. London: Department for Education and Skills. Retrieved from: www.dfes.gov.uk/research/data/uploadfiles/RR711_.pdf.

Trudell, B. & Schroeder, L. (2007) Reading Methodologies for African Languages: Avoiding Linguistic and Pedagogical Imperialism. *Language, Culture and Curriculum* 20 (3): 165.

Tse, D. (2000) *Bilingualism in British Theatre*. Blueprint Conference on Bilingualism and Theatre for Young People, Half Moon Theatre, London.

US General Accounting Office (1987) *Bilingual Education: A New Look at the Research Evidence*. U.S. General Accounting Office, Washington, DC.

Van der Avoird, T., Broeder, P. & Extra, G. (2001) Immigrant Minority Languages in the Netherlands. In G. Extra & D. Gorter (eds) *The Other Languages of Europe: Demographic, Sociolinguistic and Educational Perspectives*. Clevedon: Multilingual Matters, pp. 215–42.

Vertovec, S. (2006) *The Emergence of Super-Diversity in Britain*. Working Paper No. 25. Centre for Migration, Policy and Society, University of Oxford. Retrieved from: www.compas.ox.ac.uk/publications/papers/Steven%20Vertovec%20WP0625.pdf.

Wagner, D. (1993) *Literacy, Culture and Development: Becoming Literate in Morocco*. Cambridge: Cambridge University Press.

Wagner, D. (1999) Literacy and Development: Rationales, Myths, Innovations, and Future Directions. *International Journal of Educational Development* 15 (4): 341–62.

Wild, A. (2000) *The East India Company: Trade and Conquest from 1600*. Guilford, CT: Lyons Press.

Williams, H.A. (2007) *Self-Taught: African American Education in Slavery and Freedom*. Raleigh, NC: University of North Carolina Press.

Wolk, S, & Schildroth, A. (1986) Deaf Children and Speech Intelligibility: A National Study. In: A. Schildroth & M. Karchmer (eds) *Deaf Children in America*. San Diego, CA: College-Hill Press, pp. 139–60.

Wright, S. (2004) *Language Policy and Language Planning: From Nationalism to Globalization.* Basingstoke: Macmillan Palgrave.

Wright, W. (2005) *Evolution of Federal Policy and Implications of No Child Left Behind for Language Minority Students.* Tempe, AZ: Language Policy Research Unit (LPRU), Arizona State University.

Index